Athlone French Poets

PAUL VALERY

Athlone French Poets

General Editor EILEEN LE BRETON
*Reader in French Language and Literature,
Bedford College, University of London*

Monographs

GERARD DE NERVAL
THEOPHILE GAUTIER
VERLAINE
JULES LAFORGUE
PAUL VALERY
GUILLAUME APOLLINAIRE
SAINT-JOHN PERSE
HENRI MICHAUX

Critical Editions

VICTOR HUGO : CHATIMENTS
GERARD DE NERVAL : LES CHIMERES
ALFRED DE MUSSET : CONTES D'ESPAGNE ET D'ITALIE
THEOPHILE GAUTIER : POESIES
PAUL VERLAINE : SAGESSE
PAUL VERLAINE : ROMANCES SANS PAROLES
ARTHUR RIMBAUD : LES ILLUMINATIONS
JULES LAFORGUE : LES COMPLAINTES
PAUL VALERY : CHARMES OU POEMES
GUILLAUME APOLLINAIRE : ALCOOLS
SAINT-JOHN PERSE : EXIL
MICHAUX : AU PAYS DE LA MAGIE

PAUL VALERY

by

CHARLES G. WHITING

UNIVERSITY OF LONDON
THE ATHLONE PRESS
1978

Published by
THE ATHLONE PRESS
UNIVERSITY OF LONDON
at 4 Gower Street, London WC1

Distributed by
Tiptree Book Services Ltd
Tiptree, Essex

U.S.A. and Canada
Humanities Press Inc
New Jersey

Printed in Great Britain by
Western Printing Services Limited
Bristol

Athlone French Poets

General Editor EILEEN LE BRETON

This series is designed to provide students and general readers both with Monographs on important nineteenth- and twentieth-century French poets and Critical Editions of one or more representative works by these poets.

The Monographs aim at presenting the essential biographical facts while placing the poet in his social and intellectual context. They contain a detailed analysis of his poetical works and, where appropriate, a brief account of his other writings. His literary reputation is examined and his contribution to the development of French poetry is assessed, as is also his impact on other literatures. A selection of critical views and a bibliography are appended.

The Critical Editions contain a substantial introduction aimed at presenting each work against its historical background as well as studying its genre, structure, themes, style, etc. and highlighting its relevance for today. The text normally given is the complete text of the original edition. It is followed by full commentaries on the poems and annotation of the text, including variant readings when these are of real significance.

E. Le B.

PREFACE

After a period of eclipse such as often follows the death of a great literary figure, Valéry has been the subject of great interest for at least a decade. He has drawn the attention of both the New Novelists in France and the Structuralist critics, in large part because he extended speculation about the formal aspects of literature to its extreme point. There is also an active continuing interest in Valéry from the point of view of more traditional literary history because, as T. S. Eliot pointed out, he is the last great representative of the French Symbolist movement which began with Baudelaire. In this brief introduction to Valéry, I have given first priority to a study of his poetry and his ideas on poetry. There is also, however, an analysis of all his best-known works in prose as well as a chapter devoted to his reactions to the modern world. Finally, I have chosen to give substantial space to a presentation of the major ideas in each section of Valéry's *Cahiers*, extensive private notes made over a period of fifty years and which he himself considered his most important work. Students and other readers will find here a background to assist them in further reading in Valéry's poetry, essays, dialogues, and other works.

C.G.W.

CONTENTS

NOTE

Throughout the text, reference is made to Paul Valéry, *Œuvres* I and II, edited by Jean Hytier, Bibliothèque de la Pléiade, 1957 and 1960. These references appear in the abbreviated form, O.I and O.II. All references to the *Cahiers* are from the two volume edition in the Bibliothèque de la Pléiade, edited by Judith Robinson in 1973 and 1974.

I

BIOGRAPHY

Paul Valéry, whose ancestry was Italian on his mother's side and Corsican on his father's, was born on 30 October 1871 in the small Mediterranean seaport of Sète. He began his schooling in Sète and later studied law at the University of Montpellier where the family had moved in 1884, but he was bored by his teachers and his studies,[1] and all his life his vigorous and independent mind educated itself rather than drawing benefit from formal schooling:

J'ai dû commencer vers l'âge de neuf ou dix ans à me faire une sorte d'île de mon esprit, et quoique d'un naturel assez sociable et communicatif, je me réservais de plus en plus un jardin très secret où je cultivais les images qui me semblaient tout à fait miennes, ne pouvaient être que miennes. (O.I, pp. 13-14)

He did, however, emphasize the importance of his strong memories of a Mediterranean childhood, of brilliant sunlight and the sea where he loved to swim, at Palavas near Montpellier, and also in Italy where he went for visits with his mother's family.

On his own, the young Valéry pursued interests which were to remain with him all his life, poetry, painting, and architecture. He made pen and pencil sketches and watercolours, read Gautier, Baudelaire and Hugo, and began writing poems himself in 1884. On 15 August 1889, his first poem was published in *La Petite Revue Maritime* of Marseilles. It was entitled 'Rêve' (O.I, p. 1573), and had been sent to the review by Valéry's older brother, Jules, later to become an eminent jurist. By the time he was 19, Valéry had written between two and three hundred poems.[2]

A friend, Pierre Féline, who lived in the same building as Valéry in Montpellier in 1889, guided his interest in mathematics, physics and music, Beethoven and above all Wagner, for whom Valéry was always to have unbounded admiration.[3] Then on 20 May 1890, at Palavas, during the celebration of the six hundredth anniversary of the University of Montpellier, an extraordinary meeting took place. Through pure chance, the young Valéry met Pierre Louÿs, a young Symbolist poet and editor who helped

introduce Valéry to literary figures in Paris, and who published
several of Valéry's early poems in *La Conque*. Through Louÿs,
Valéry met the young André Gide, who came to Montpellier late
in 1890 to visit his uncle, the jurist Charles Gide, and who read
Valéry some pages of the *Cahiers d'André Walter*. The friendship
with Gide lasted over fifty years with an important and voluminous
correspondence.[4] It was also through Pierre Louÿs that Valéry
was able to meet Mallarmé in Paris in the autumn of 1891. Valéry
had first discovered Mallarmé, as well as Verlaine and the
Goncourt brothers in 1889, by reading Huysman's *A Rebours*, a
book he read and re-read. After the first meeting with Pierre
Louÿs, Valéry wrote to him that he had only been able to read
those parts of Mallarmé's 'Hérodiade' which had appeared in *A
Rebours*, and so on 22 September 1890, Louÿs sent Valéry 30
lines of 'Hérodiade', copied out in his elegant handwriting. On
20 October, Valéry wrote to Mallarmé for the first time, enclosing
two short poems, 'Le Jeune Prêtre' (O.I, p. 1578) and 'La Suave
Agonie'' (O.I, pp. 1581–2). Immediately Mallarmé answered
him: 'Le don de subtile analogie, avec la musique adéquate,
vous possédez cela qui est tout . . . Quant à des conseils, seule en
donne la solitude. . .' Early in 1891, Valéry again wrote Mallarmé,
who replied: 'Votre "Narcisse Parle" me charme . . . Gardez ce
ton rare. . .'

In *Propos Me Concernant*, Valéry has recalled the powerful
effect that the discovery of Mallarmé, and then of Rimbaud had
upon him in late 1889.[5] He was profoundly marked by his contact with Mallarmé, and for the rest of his life he had a cult for
this great Symbolist poet.[6] From the first contact with Mallarmé's
poetry, Valéry was aware of its absolute quality, its mastery of
language and a formal perfection which made all other poetry
seem inferior.

But Mallarmé's influence, in conjunction with that of Edgar
Allan Poe, had also an effect on Valéry quite contrary to the
pursuit of poetry.[7] Valéry's interest turned toward the mind
which had made these marvellous verbal combinations possible.
Poe's influence was even greater than that of Mallarmé. If
Mallarmé launched Valéry in his important life-long interest in
language, Poe stimulated his interest in science and the intellect,
in that 'self-consciousness' which was a path toward the *Moi Pur*,

pure intellectual functioning always detaching itself from everything (*Cahiers* I, pp. 317–18).[8] Poe's emphasis on the importance
of method and lucidity, as well as a remark in *Arnheim* that man
was far from having realized in any field the perfection he could
reach, combined to encourage further Valéry's ambition to
master as far as was humanly possible the operations of the mind.
At the same time, Valéry was also influenced by Poe's theory of
poetry, which was a psychological rather than an aesthetic
theory, stressing the creation of effects in the minds of readers.
Such speculations finally seemed to Valéry to require a 'sacrifice
of the intellect' and more and more poetry, once so venerated,
seemed a secondary occupation of the mind.

In 1892, Valéry was the victim of a *crise sentimentale*, an intense
passion for a married woman, a certain Madame de Rovira with
whom he had hardly any contact and to whom he never made
any declaration of love. The importance of this ravaging passion,
however, should not be underestimated; it led to the famous 'nuit
de Gênes', 4–5 October 1892, when Valéry determined that he
would not let himself be dominated by his unusual capacity for
intense feelings, and also resolved to turn away from literature in
order to study the mind.[9] On the other hand, it should be clear
from the preceding discussion that this turning-point in Valéry's
life was not merely a sudden change provoked by unhappy love,
but the culmination of tendencies which had been forming within
him for some time, tendencies favoured not only by the influence
of Mallarmé and Poe but also by the climate of the last decades
of the nineteenth century when young French intellectuals,
reacting to the defeat of France in the Franco-Prussian War of
1870–1, to the influence of Barrès and the 'culte du moi', and
against the realistic and naturalistic novel and the objective and
descriptive poetry of the Parnassian school, were turning inward
toward the self.[10] The abandonment of literature, however,
should not be imagined as something absolute and total. As we
shall see, in many ways Valéry maintained contacts with literature
in the period following 1892. Still, there can be no question about
the decisive turning away from the idea that poetry represented
the finest cultivation of the mind and the path to wisdom and
revelation.

Now, instead of being dominated by his sensibility, Valéry

decided to master it by turning it into an object for rational scrutiny: 'Etre à soi son Grand Capitaine, son calculateur propre d'élans, de folies, d'extrêmes douceurs apparemment incalculables.'[11] He had made a great discovery: the mind is a 'système fermé', a closed system creating its images and ideas from sense data, and whose images and ideas have a purely intellectual existence not to be confused with things and 'reality'.[12] His ambition was to discover the possibilities of this system, its potentialities and limits, to develop his powers as much as possible, to 'reconstruct' his mind,[13] to master it, 'possess' it, but without attempting to use it in some particular career.[14] From the beginning, Valéry was not only remarkably strong-willed but also unusually lucid about himself. In 1894 he wrote to Gide: 'J'ai agi toujours pour me rendre un individu potentiel. C'est-à-dire que j'ai préféré une vie stratégique à une tactique. Avoir à ma disposition sans disposer' (*Correspondance Gide-Valéry*, pp. 217–18).

A parallel with Descartes is apparent in Valéry's affirmation of intellectual independence, in his characteristic 'nettoyage de la pensée' and founding of all knowledge and certainty on the self, in his scrupulous attachment to rigorous method, and above all in his ambition for reducing the processes of the mind to measurable quantities. He was reading, in this last decade of the nineteenth century, the works of the physicists Clerk Maxwell and Lord Kelvin, and of the German mathematician Georg Cantor, and especially the books of the great French mathematician Henri Poincaré, who so stressed the importance of form and of relationships between things, and whose influence is clearly visible in Valéry's first major essay, 'Introduction à la Méthode de Léonard de Vinci'. On 3 March 1894, Valéry left Montpellier for Paris, where he lived in the rue Gay-Lussac in a severe little room having as its chief object a blackboard which he covered with equations and calculations, and he wrote to Gide: 'Aujourd'hui tout *doit* venir de moi. Je n'admets rien que je ne comprenne et je traduis le mot travail par trouvaille. Apprendre, lire, peiner sur la pièce, n'est pas travail pour moi. Je me croirais un paresseux d'écrire des encyclopédies, car écrire en lui-même ou feuilleter, c'est un prétexte pour ne rien *trouver*' (idem, p. 209).

It should not be thought, however, that Valéry in emphasizing the intellect never included any role for the body or the unconscious. The body, as will be very clear in the dialogue 'Eupalinos' in 1921 is the indispensable servant of the mind and its necessary contact with concrete reality. What Valéry does rebel against are the hampering and constraining influences on the functioning of the mind, those repetitive, cyclical aspects of existence which seem so foreign to the intellect and which will be dramatically opposed to it in Valéry's great poem of 1917, *La Jeune Parque*.[15] As for the unconscious, Christine Crow has summed up Valéry's attitude toward it with the statement that the ' "Apollonian" orientation of Valéry's thought is never mere rationalism',[16] and much of her book is devoted to showing that Valéry had a vision of mental unity, including both rational and irrational, conscious and unconscious processes. This unity, however, was to be finally directed and governed as much as possible by reason, and never by the irrational.[17] It is significant, for example, that if Valéry was all his life interested in religion, even in mystical and visionary writings, he remained an atheist.[18]

In 1894, the same year Valéry moved into his little room in the rue Gay-Lussac, he began the *Cahiers*, private notebooks where he wrote brief developments of disconnected ideas on certain problems which interested him. In 1922, referring to those notes in a letter to Gide, he wrote: 'Mon vrai moi est là' (idem, p. 493). He continued writing in these notebooks until his death in 1945, filling in all some 29,000 pages. Valéry got up at 4 a.m. each morning, made himself coffee, smoked a few cigarettes, and worked alone and in peace for several hours writing down these ideas which were not intended for publication, although he did publish some of them during his lifetime, drew on them for his published essays, and in 1908 made a first attempt at classifying them.[19] Just before his death in 1945, Valéry said to Gide: 'Les principaux thèmes autour desquels j'ai ordonné ma pensée depuis cinquante ans demeurent pour moi INEBRANLABLES!' and Gide added this comment: 'Il disait ce dernier mot en accentuant fortement chaque syllabe'.[20] Valéry had many of his insights early in life, and they were enriched, rather than dramatically varied by the passage of time.

Valéry's interests during his so-called 'Silence' from 1892 to 1917 were not entirely monopolized by a study of the intellect and related matters. For one thing, he was not at all unaware of what was happening in the world around him. He was particularly concerned with the destiny of Europe vis-à-vis emerging non-European powers such as Japan in its war with China in 1895, and the United States against Spain in 1898, and he was preoccupied also by the internal politics of Europe, the negative effects of traditional enmities, and the threat of modern Germany. On this last matter, he wrote the prophetic 'La Conquête Allemande', published in England in *The New Review* in January 1897 and later reprinted in the *Mercure de France*, 1 September 1915 (O.I, pp. 971–87), as a conclusion drawn from the study of Ernest E. Williams entitled *Made in Germany*.[21] Valéry was also maintaining his contact with literature. The *Cahiers* themselves show no rejection of an interest in poetry; on the contary they contain numerous reflections on poetry and on Poe, Mallarmé and Rimbaud as well as fragments of 'poésie brute 'and sketches of possible writings. Throughout the 'Silence' there was a frequent output of un-published prose and verse and short prose poems. Between 1892 and 1900 Valéry still appeared in print. In 1895 he published his famous essay, 'Introduction à la Méthode de Léonard de Vinci', in 1896 the poems 'Eté' and 'Vue', and the extraordinary 'Soirée avec Monsieur Teste', while in 1897 he participated in an homage to Mallarmé with the charming poem 'Valvins' (name of the village where Mallarmé lived), published 'La Conquête Allemande' mentioned above, and began a series of three articles under the significant title 'Méthodes' which appeared in the *Mercure de France* in 1897, 1898 and 1899 (O.II, pp. 1446–60). In 1898 he also published an article on Huysmans entitled 'Durtal' and in 1900 the poem 'Anne'. After 1900 there was much less publication, still, the brief 'L'Amateur de poèmes' should be noted in 1906 and the 'Etudes et fragments sur le rêve' in 1909. Further-more, during this period of 'Silence', Valéry was not at all absent from the literary and artistic world of Paris. He continued to see Mallarmé until his death in 1898,[22] and was a regular figure at the 'mardis' of the Rue de Rome where he met many of the young poets of the day. He maintained his friendship with Gide and Louÿs, and also with Heredia, Hérold, Fontainas, Viélé-Griffin, Huysmans, and Marcel Schwob. In 1894 he met and talked with George Meredith in England and wrote to Gide about his fascination with the spectacle of commerce in the City. He added:

'A l'époque récente où je lisais, étudiais, et faisais des vers, je me serais coupé la langue plutôt que de penser et de dire cela' (*idem*, p. 209). He went to the first performance of Jarry's *Ubu Roi*, regularly attended the Concerts Lamoureux, met Degas in 1896 and wished to dedicate 'La Soirée avec Monsieur Teste' to him (Degas refused.) In 1896 Valéry was one of those who went to Verlaine's funeral. Thus it is clear that although Valéry's major interests had most certainly changed after 1892, there never was any break in his interest in literature between 1892 and 1912 when he began working on *La Jeune Parque*.

In 1896 he was in London working for the press service of the Chartered Company, translating articles on South Africa. In 1895, on the advice of Huysmans, Valéry had taken the civil service examination for the post of clerk in the War Ministry, where he began work on May 1897. These new duties left him little time or energy for his own research.[23] In late 1898 he met Jeannie Gobillard, the niece of the painter Berthe Morisot, and became engaged to her in early 1900. 'Degas a brusqué les choses en dernier lieu et dans son atelier ont été dites les paroles définitives' (*Correspondance Valéry-Fourment*, p. 156). He was married on 31 May 1900 with André Gide and Pierre Louÿs as witnesses. In July he left the War Ministry to become a sort of private secretary to Edouard Lebey of the Havas Agency, a post in which he remained for twenty-two years and which only required three or four hours work a day, thus leaving him considerable free time for his personal work.[24] Valéry's marriage further strengthened his ties with the world of art. In the next few years he met and conversed with a number of the greatest painters of the late nineteenth and early twentieth centuries, amongst them Renoir, Monet, Redon and Vuillard. Impressionist painting, however, had not much appeal for Valéry because he found in it little of the intellectual content he demanded of art, little evidence of critical and compositional faculties in the artist. Beginning with the Romantics of the early nineteenth century, Valéry saw a progressive decline in the seriousness, solemnity and intellectual content of painting. He did respect Delacroix, however, as a great theorist, and Daumier for his abilities as satirist and moralist. He was unwilling to class Corot as an intellectual, but recognized that at least he composed his landscapes. Among his contemporaries, Valéry particularly admired Degas, the very model of the artist directed by intellect and strength of will.[25]

Valéry also knew the sculptor Rodin and the architect Auguste Perret. He met the poets Saint-John Perse and P.-J. Toulet, the great theatre director Jacques Copeau, and the composers Debussy and Ravel. His strongest tastes in music, however, were for Gluck and above all for Wagner, both of whom were to have an influence on *La Jeune Parque*. Wagner kept the attraction of artistic creation alive in Valéry's mind, as is evident in an important letter from 1908: 'Telle que je vois son œuvre, elle m'apparaît la seule entreprise dans l'art moderne qui conserve l'équilibre des facultés diverses à exciter dans l'homme et qui en exige la connaissance et l'instinct dans l'auteur' (O.I, p. 32). In 1912, Valéry yielded to the urgings of Gide and Gallimard that he should publish a collection of his poetry and prose.[26] First, however, he wished to revise his old verses and add others for publication, and these new verses, intended to be a forty-line farewell to poetry, became *La Jeune Parque*. Still, his major interest was the study of the intellect, and he viewed the writing of poetry as a means for both training and observing the mind.[27] A very important letter from 1915 to Albert Coste defines his intellectual activity:

Tout ce qu'il y a de moins métaphysicien, ce que j'ai essaye constamment à travers mille variations de sujets et de procédés, le voici : Introduire dans ma pensée, quelle qu'elle soit, le souci de la rigueur, et la conscience d'elle-même; acquérir le plus de liberté, à moi possible, de combinaison et de dissociation; éviter avec soin la confusion (que l'usage et le langage admettent et imposent) entre les fictions et les vrais actes psychiques, entre le vu, le pensé, le raisonné, le senti; placer dans ces manœuvres et précautions intérieures l'essentiel, l'important par excellence, et retirer cette importance aux intuitions et aux jugements mêmes, toujours provisoires. Pour moi, une représentation ou 'idée' du Monde (s'il existe) si on la veut aussi exacte et fine que chacun la peut comporter, doit être précédée et dérivée de cette Ethique ... sportive... Ma 'philosophie', vous le voyez, est individuelle. Elle m'implique tel quel, explicitement. Elle tend donc à une organisation finie, non à une explication ou construction des choses. Méthode plus que système. Méthodes plus que méthode. (*Lettres à Quelques-Uns*, p. 106, pp. 108–9)

Valéry's creative powers had gathered strength from the

intellectual activities of the period of 'Silence', and these powers, combined with nearly five years of hard work, produced *La Jeune Parque*, published on 30 April 1917.[28] This magnificent long poem, remarkable not only for its incantatory beauty, its élan toward heroism, but also for its extraordinary imagery of the life of the body, made Valéry famous throughout Europe.[29] It remains today as no doubt the greatest long poem in French of the twentieth century. As Valéry himself said wittily: 'Son obscurité me mit en lumière' (O.I, p. 39). If in the early 1890s poetry was too rare and exalted to be the object of a career, now in 1917 and until the end of his life it was to remain something ambivalent, beloved and yet also suspect. In *Propos Me Concernant*, Valéry explains his objections to poetry:

J'ai fait de la *littérature* en homme qui, au fond, ne l'aime pas trop pour elle-même — puisqu'il y trouve la nécessité de rechercher des 'effets', d'employer des moyens à étonner et exciter la superficie de l'esprit — (si l'on veut aller plus avant, le lecteur *casse*; et l'auteur lui-même s'embarrasse.) La qualité de l'attention littéraire n'est pas la qualité d'attention qui me séduit. (O.II, p. 1521)

Always Valéry felt a longing for a purely private and disinterested rumination of his ideas, detached from any public career of publication. In a 1927 letter he wrote: 'J'étais créé pour m'amuser avec mes idées le matin, bavarder le soir, et point écrire.'[30] Still, this complex man was also a great poet with a genius for the manipulation of language, and he did write and publish, 'Le Cimetière Marin' and the *Album de Vers Anciens* in 1920, then the great collection of *Charmes* in 1922 with its variety of forms and tones, ranging from the witty burlesque passages and linguistic inventions of 'Ebauche d'un Serpent' to the incantatory charm of 'Fragment du Narcisse'. After the 1926 edition of *Charmes*, however, with its addition of two further sections to 'Fragments du Narcisse', Valéry's public career as a poet was over. There were no further great collections. We know, however, that his poetic activity did not cease, and recently it has been revealed that this private production was very different in manner from *La Jeune Parque* and *Charmes*, short prose poems closer to contemporary poetry, and poems in verse filled with a natural flow of lyrical feeling. Also, apparently in almost every period of his life, Valéry wrote brief erotic poems, *Carmina eroticissima*, and

the eventual publication of what is still unedited may alter somewhat our idea of Valéry as poet.

Very practical reasons also obliged Valéry to write and publish.
On 14 February 1922, his employer Edouard Lebey died, leaving
Valéry with no regular source of income. Valéry then had no
recourse but to live by his pen, and as he remarked to Gide in
1929, he had never 'rien écrit que sur commande et pressé par le
besoin d'argent'.[31] He became the brilliant essayist of the period
between the two world wars, producing articles on literature,
philosophy, art, and the modern world, numerous prefaces, and
he lectured all over Europe. Probably nothing he ever wrote
became more widely known than the two letters entitled 'La
Crise de l'Esprit', first published in England in *The Athenæum* and
then in *Nouvelle Revue Française* in France in 1919 (O.I, pp. 988–
1000), or rather it was the first sentence of these letters which
became famous: 'Nous autres, civilisations, nous savons maintenant que nous sommes mortelles.' Valéry, so little a part of the
major literary and artistic currents of the new century, became
one of the first prophetic voices in France to analyse the period of
crisis which followed the first world war. The twenties were to
see new forms of art, notably Surrealism, an interest in far-off
civilizations in Africa and the Pacific, and above all a great
questioning of traditional values, stimulated by the influence of
Nietzsche, Dostoievski, Freud, Bergson, and carried out not only
by such great contemporaries of Valéry as André Gide, but also
by the young Surrealists and by André Malraux in such texts as
La Tentation de l'Occident in 1926 and *D'une Jeunesse Européenne* in
1927.

Valéry also questioned accepted moral codes and the usual
practices of criminal justice (see *Cahiers*: 'Homo'), as well as the
weaknesses of the French political system (see *Cahiers*: 'Histoire-
Politique'), and already in 'La Crise de l'Esprit' he recognized
that the twentieth century was characterized by a departure from
old traditions and by the co-existence of opposed ideas. He was,
however, less interested in undermining the traditions of society
than in analysing and criticizing what was new in the world
following the first world war. Too attached to his own æsthetic
ideas, he remained closed to modern art, painting, architecture,
literature and the cinema, which he criticized for their facility,

shock-effects and obsession with novelty. His alert intelligence, however, saw lucidly the problems of the modern world and one of his major preoccupations was the decline of Europe. Against that decline, the most important remedy he envisaged was the creation of a united continent rejecting the outmoded spirit of nationalism.

He was among the first to see that the complexities of society, its technological refinement, its continual creation and satisfaction of new needs, could become increasingly opposed to the simple original needs of man, and that what was considered progress could really be debilitating. So sensitive to the idea of the integrity of the individual, Valéry complained that the modern world required 'organization men' at all levels of the economy: workers on a production line, and managers with more obedience to a system and hierarchy than originality and initiative. Even modern science, a particular interest of Valéry's, was suspect. It had helped to create the destructive machines of war.

At no time, however, did Valéry lose faith in the intelligence. In 1919, he wrote 'Note et Digression' (O.I, pp. 1199–233), presenting the MOI PUR, intellectual functioning ever exhausting new problems and challenges and maintaining its purity by its refusals and rejections, a powerful response to those limits to the mind which this essay also explores. In 1932, the dialogue *L'Idée Fixe* again offers the same opposition of limits and strengths, here in the person of Robinson Crusoe, Valéry's myth of the independent creative thinker (O.II, pp. 195–275). If 'Note et Digression' seems inhuman in its striving toward an intellectual Absolute, the dialogue 'Eupalinos', which followed in 1921, rejects the Absolute and embraces the vicissitudes of life and the marvellous human body (O.II, pp. 79–147). It does this, however, in the interests of architectural construction, the powerful charm of great art, and re-construction of the artist's mind. A second dialogue, also written in 1921, 'L'Ame et la Danse', offers still another perspective on the *Moi Pur* and 'life' (O.II, pp. 148–76). Here Valéry suggests that the clairvoyance of the rigorous intelligence at times reveals life in all its cruel reality, producing in the thinker an overwhelming *ennui de vivre*. Again, as in 'Eupalinos', it is the creative action of art which elevates man and even permits a fleeting contact with the Absolute in a moment of perfect self-possession. There is then a certain relationship between the 'inhuman rejections' of 'La Soirée avec Monsieur Teste' and the 'Note et Digression', and the 'acceptances' of 'Eupalinos' and 'L'Ame et la Danse'. These were Valéry's greatest prose creations in the period between the two world wars. At no time did he consider writing novels, a genre he felt absolutely foreign to his tastes. Valéry always identified the novel with Naturalism, which he had rejected as a young man, and unjustly believed all novels to be nothing more than a facile copy of trivial quotidian events, lacking that rigour, calculation, and composition which he, the supremely self-conscious artist, demanded of art. Stendhal is the only major novelist to whom he accorded an important essay.[32]

Valéry was at the same time an egocentric and very isolated and independent artist and thinker, but also an extremely sociable person, a brilliant conversationalist, and a man who had experienced great friendships,[33] who felt passion for women, and tenderness for his three children. Attachment to his family no doubt explains the abrupt ending to a first great love affair with Catherine Pozzi on 23 October 1921. She was a gifted young married woman, the daughter of a famous surgeon, a woman with whom Valéry felt he could have a complete and ideal relationship, emotional, physical, and intellectual.[34] It is a rather different attitude toward love from the one he had exhibited after the 'crise sentimentale' of 1892, and after this first affair in 1920–1, we find him searching the rest of his life for an ideal relationship. There was a second affair with the sculptress Renée Vautier which seems to have ended in 1932 and is no doubt referred to in *L'Idée Fixe*, and then a final liaison in the last years of his life. The unfinished play 'Lust' in Valéry's *Mon Faust* remains as a testimony of his longing for a perfect communion he never found.

Launched by *La Jeune Parque* and *Charmes*, Valéry frequented the salons of Paris, travelled abroad, and met such literary figures and critics as Conrad, T. S. Eliot, D'Annunzio, Rilke, Stefan Zweig, Ortega y Gasset, Pirandello, and Bernard Berenson. He had discussions with Bergson and Teilhard de Chardin, and knew Honegger and Stravinsky. He also met military figures, Pétain and Foch, and talked with several of the most prominent French political leaders, Briand, Blum, and Herriot. These conversations as well as worsening events were instrumental in cultivating in Valéry an increasing attention to world problems from 1929 until the end of his life. The conversations which most fascinated Valéry, however, in this *période mondaine*, were no doubt those he had with great mathematicians and physicists, Louis de Broglie, Paul Langevin, Jacques Hadamard, Frédéric Joliot-Curie, and Einstein, in whom Valéry had been interested since 1915. He had pursued the study of science and mathematics since the 1890s and he was well-informed of the state of modern science, better certainly than most of his contemporaries.

Now that he was an acclaimed public figure, Valéry received a series of honours. On 17 March 1921 in a poll conducted by the review *Connaissance,* he was chosen as the greatest living poet. In 1924 he was elected president of the P.E.N. Club, and on 19 November 1925 to the French Academy. In 1926 he was participating as a member of the Committee on Intellectual Cooperation of the League of Nations, and in 1933 the French Government selected him as administrator of the Centre Universitaire Méditerranéen at Nice. He became a member of the Academy of Sciences of Lisbon in 1935, and received honorary degrees from Coimbra and from Oxford. In 1937, he was elected to a Chair of Poetics at the Collège de France, which gave him the opportunity to elucidate further his ideas on poetry.[35]

When the second world war broke out Valéry was still teaching at the Collège de France. Shortly after the invasion of France by the German armies in May 1940, he reluctantly left Paris for Brittany, where he began work on *Mon Faust* during the summer. In September he returned again to Paris. Valéry had long been critical of the disorder and incoherence of French democracy and he had several times criticized a political system which he felt crushed individual initiatives. Despite his intensified interest in world politics in the 1930s, however, he had always refused to enter the French political arena, seeing it as destructive of the intellectual values he sought to preserve.[36] Still, it is moving to recall to what extent Valéry's attitudes during the Occupation and after the Liberation were positive and admirable, even noble, and in no way anti-democratic. He was Gaullist, pro-English, and one of the first opponents of Vichy, although he had been a friend of Pétain and had given the speech receiving him into the

French Academy. In 1941 Valéry had the moral courage to speak at the Academy in praise of the great Jewish philosopher Bergson, who had died in January. Vichy, aware of his opinions, removed him from his functions at the Centre Universitaire Méditerranéen in the same year, and in 1942 the German authorities refused paper for the publication of Valéry's *Mauvaises Pensées*, asking 'Pourquoi n'écrit-il pas les Bonnes?' (O.I, p. 69). (At a later date the authorization was finally given.) In spite of this, with characteristic generosity of spirit, Valéry intervened personally after the Liberation on behalf of Maurras, Brasillach and Bérard, accused of collaboration with the enemy.

In the spring of 1945 Valéry was suffering terribly from cancer, and on 20 July 1945 he died, aged nearly 74. General de Gaulle requested a state funeral, and on 24 July the coffin was carried from the Place Victor Hugo to the Trocadéro and placed on a catafalque draped with the colours of France, with students holding vigil and the crowd filing past all night. During the night, the Pantheon, a monument which contains the remains of many of France's greatest men, was the only public building in Paris which remained illuminated. On 27 July, Paul Valéry was buried in the cemetery at Sète which was the scene of one of his greatest poems, and on his tomb two lines from the first stanza of 'Le Cimetière Marin' were engraved:

> O récompense après une pensée
> Qu'un long regard sur le calme des dieux!

POETRY

EARLY POETRY[1]

Over sixty poems, written between 1884 and 1899, are available to us from the period of Valéry's youth. Many appeared in various Symbolist reviews such as *La Syrinx*, *La Plume*, *La Wallonie*, *La Conque*, others were never published. In 1920 Valéry gathered a selection of his early poems in *Album de Vers Anciens*, where, however, they were much revised. Furthermore, it has become apparent that three of the *Album* poems, 'César', 'Air de Sémiramis', and 'Profusion du Soir' are not early works at all. The first two were composed at the time that Valéry was writing the poems of *Charmes*, while 'Profusion du Soir', added to the 1926 edition of his *Album*, was written after 1922. Recently, however, an original draft for 'Air de Sémiramis' has come to light,[2] dating from the very end of Valéry's early period, and we will use this draft to indicate important developments in Valéry's early poetry. Our purpose, in this chapter, is not so much to examine the early poems for themselves, although their charm is undeniable, as to offer some indications on how they evolve toward the poetry of *La Jeune Parque* and *Charmes*. Without making any exaggerated claims for the early production, it is certain that there are many more links between it and Valéry's great period than may be immediately apparent.

First of all, a few general remarks should be made. It is clear that the younger Valéry was already attached to regular prosody, since most of the early poems are sonnets. And many of Valéry's early verses already contain a striking musicality, for example the opening lines of 'La Fileuse': 'Assise la fileuse au bleu de la croisée / Où le Jardin mélodieux se dodeline' (O.I, p. 1534), where the incantatory quality is far greater than in the poems of most of Valéry's young contemporaries. 'La Fileuse' is also an example of the evident elevation of themes in these early poems. Few of them are devoted to ordinary everyday happenings. 'Repas' (O.I, p. 1593), written in 1889, is a rare example of a sonnet in a Verlainian minor key, sketching a small and insignificant event. 'Episode' (O.I, pp. 83–4), published in 1892, which evokes a trivial flirtation, is elevated by a refined pastoral atmosphere, by precious sensuality and elegance, and by the musical charm of the lines. Usually the themes are even more obviously justified. Valéry deals with legendary poets, pure beauty, heroic antiquity, the creation of form. In this respect, he will not change when he later writes the poems of *Charmes*, where even poems which appear merely witty and flippant, such as 'Le Sylphe', are removed from everyday existence and always have deep significance.

The predominating theme in the early period is 'voyance', mystical flight from a quotidian world to some superior state. It is a magical transformation accomplished through dreams, or religious emotions, through a sea-voyage to an exotic port, through death, and in some poems by the emotion of friendship. 'Le Bois Amical' (O.I, p. 80) is no doubt the best of the friendship poems: two friends walk together at night, holding hands, and finally, at a high point of emotion, they die and are transported to the stars above. That the friendship poems were not merely poetic exercises becomes evident through a reading of Valéry's correspondence:

J'ai fréquenté tous mes amis dans le dessein de leur offrir quelque jour une suprême fiançaille, une expérience d'apothéose. Nul n'y a vu une des cimes humaines, ni deviné le rayonnement de l'amicale condensation et que cela contenait un recommencement du Monde et des fleurs. Alas! il n'y a plus Personne qui veuille fixement affronter l'Impossible, se dévouer au plaisir divin, faire le soleil.[3]

In the first seven stanzas of 'Le Cimetière Marin' in *Charmes*, the 'voyance' theme will appear again, but with two major changes. First, it will become explicitly an intellectual transformation, a purification of the intellect, while the old theme of death and passage to paradise of such early poems as 'La Suave Agonie' (O.I, pp. 1581–2) is mocked as 'songes vains' (l. 66). Then, purity for the poet, either in life or death, is revealed as a tragic impossibility. But already in 1899, in his draft of 'Air de Sémiramis', Valéry attributed intellectual omnipotence not to himself but to a legendary heroine, to an ideal figure like his Leonardo. Here the flight-image is represented by the emergence of the queen on a high suspended bridge where she can survey all of Babylon. Solitude, height, and far vision are aspects of a powerful dominating intellect, and she looks down with pride and contempt on the tiny beings she dominates. Even in 1890 there were hints of the direction the flight-theme might take in the introspective poem 'Conseil d'Ami' (O.I, p. 1590), where the poet closes his door to mistresses and takes refuge within the self, and also in the significant 1889 poem 'Les Chats Blancs' (O.I, p. 1594), with its proud turning-inward toward thought and intellectual clarity. At the same time, certain very early poems of heroic action quite different from Valéry's usual inspiration, poems such as 'La Marche Impériale' (p. 1575), evoking a pagan victory parade, or 'Le Jeune Prêtre' (p. 1578) with a cosmic battle scene, or 'Hélène, la reine triste' (p. 76) and its legendary warriors, seem to prefigure the forceful heroic qualities of 'Air de Sémiramis', *La Jeune Parque* and 'Le Cimetière Marin'.

Whilst there is an evolution of the flight-theme in the early poetry, there is also an important evolution of imagery. In the early flight-poems, the image of the protagonist is effaced, hardly visible, and his psychological and physiological reactions are non-existent or minimal. In 'La Suave Agonie' (O.I, p. 1581), a woman is dying, about to pass to some superior world, and there are images of her large dead eyes, of vague languid gestures. 'Sur l'Eau' (O.I, pp. 1594–5) which begins with the word 'Fuir!', and where the flight is a boat trip, is not much different. Again there is a sketchy image of a woman's eyes, pale features, delicate blushes, nothing more than the vague presence of a woman who seems hardly alive and who is about to disappear into oblivion. These vague presences may be surrounded by a decor of jewels and precious metals. The boat in 'Sur l'Eau' is made of 'ivoire incrusté d'argent.' But this solid elegance does not clash with the effaced protagonists because it is modified by an extensive vocabulary of refining and diminishing words such as 'fin', 'pâle', 'lent', 'calme', 'tendre', 'doux', 'taciturne', and 'vague'. If the boat of 'Sur l'Eau' is made of ivory and silver, it is also 'un canot frêle'. This imagery of precious materials, elegant and refined, may even be extended to the female figures in these poems, as in the delicate sculptural image of the very young girl in 'Blanc' (O.I, p. 1543): 'Chair de perle que moule une gaze nacrée', and

'pieds fins chaussés d'hermine et de cristal', or again in 'Les
Vaines Danseuses' (O.I, p. 80): 'Figurines d'or et beautés toutes
menues'.

Still, in two of the earlier poems, dating from 1890 and 1892,
something occurs which anticipates a radical change in the
imagery of protagonists and their surroundings. In 'Celle qui
sort de l'onde' (O.I, pp. 1541), a nymph emerges from the sea
and walks on the beach:

> Les graviers d'or qu'arrose sa marche gracile
> Croulent sous ses pieds fins et la grève facile
> Garde les frais baisers de ses pas puérils.

In 'Baignée' (O.I, p. 1545), another young girl bathes in a
fountain:

> Un bras vague, inondé dans le néant limpide
> Pour une ombre de fleur à cueillir doucement
> S'effile, ondule, oublie en le délice vide,

The sculptural details are still there, as well as the vocabulary of
elegance and refinement, 'gracile', 'fins', 'vague', 'ombre', 'or',
but there is also something new. The flesh has become truly
carnal, filled with life, capable of sensations. There has been a
movement from cold and lifeless body details toward the sensually
sculptural body of the Parque: 'îles de mon sein nu'. At the same
time the world surrounding the protagonist has changed from a
cold metallic gold to golden sand, soft and yielding, or to a
delicious pool of water.

'Celle qui sort de l'onde' and 'Baignée' are followed by 'Eté',
a poem published in 1896 with powerful sensations of summer air
and sea and imagery of the living flesh of a sleeping girl:

> Eté! roche d'air pur et toi, ardente ruche
> De mer éparpillée en mille mouches sur
> Les touffes d'une chair fraîche comme une cruche
>   (O.I, p. 1564)

She is one of three sleeping girls whose nude bodies will be
contemplated by the poet. In 'Anne' (O.I, p. 89), written in 1893,
she is a waking girl, but hardly awake, and then in 'La Dormeuse'
of *Charmes* again a half-naked girl asleep. Was Valéry drawn to
these sleeping or waking figures because they offered the op-

portunity to direct attention to the body, to its forms and its carnal existence? At the same time, sleep or drowsiness may well have been an intentional barrier between poet and woman, because sexuality is ambiguous already in the early period: if she is attractive, the woman is also dangerous.[4]

The woman in 'Anne', while not entirely awake, is not at all without developed reactions, and this is a significant departure from the sleeping princess of 'La Belle au Bois Dormant' of 1891 (O.I, p. 1546), a fleshless princess who is hardly alive and who is a sister to the vague female figures of 'La Suave Agonie' and 'Sur l'Eau'. Anne looks at her body, remembers the oblivion of sleep from which she has just emerged, appreciates her solitude and freedom from lovers, breathes in the perfume of a flower and touches the morning light with her hand. With this evolution of the protagonist, the surroundings have become 'justified'. No longer are they merely 'there' as in 'Blanc' with its ivory steps and silvery moonlight. In 'Anne' or 'Air de Sémiramis', if any element of decor is mentioned it is because the protagonist pays attention to it, reacts to it. Consequently there is no longer the highly organized and detailed setting of 'Blanc', but a partially-evoked world leaving room for the reader's imagination. And, developing no doubt from the water and sand of 'Celle qui sort le l'onde' and 'Baignée', the world of the later early poems, 'Eté', 'Vue', 'Valvins', and 'Air de Sémiramis', is no longer metallic and bejewelled but familiar: seaside scenes, a beach, port, a river, a busy city, and created by a simpler vocabulary without the rare terms of the earlier poems. But this familiar world never becomes quotidian. If Valéry no longer sets it apart with ivory and amethysts, he does remove it by purification, by distancing and by solitude. It is already an anticipation of the purified, intensely sensed, yet familiar seaside world of *La Jeune Parque* and 'Le Cimetière Marin'.

In both *La Jeune Parque* and 'Le Cimetière Marin', the purified seaside world is the scene of a dramatic monologue, and it is in the monologue that we will trace a final evolution in the early poetry. In 1891 Valéry published his first long monologue-poem, 'Narcisse Parle' (O.I, pp. 1551–2), demonstrating that the monologue form was particularly suited to his poetic genius. 'Narcisse Parle' has an effective beginning and ending, something Valéry

had difficulty achieving in many of the shorter early poems. Above
all, it creates an impression of a poetic world and an interior life:
an enchanted twilight forest inhabited by a sad and languishing
Narcissus, who nevertheless responds to the sensual beauty of his
image in the pool and to the tender suavity of nightfall. In 1896,
Valéry revised and completed a poem written sometime earlier
to create 'Eté' (O.I, pp. 1564–5) for *Le Centaure*. It too is a monologue, but less a development of interior life than a series of
sensations, reactions to the sea on a hot summer day. One of the
most striking things about the poem is its great intensity, a force
of sensation and expression distinguishing it markedly from the
weak languor of 'Narcisse Parle'.[5] At the same time as Valéry
was strengthening the protagonist and intensifying his sensations,
he was seeking ways to make the monologue more forceful.

This force persists in the elaborate draft of the monologue 'Air
de Sémiramis', where Valéry returns to an evocation of interior
life. But unlike Narcissus, Sémiramis, legendary queen and
builder of Babylon, entirely dominates the poem.[6] She is the
absolute centre of interest, like the protagonists of *La Jeune
Parque*, 'Le Cimetière Marin' and 'Fragments du Narcisse', and
the powerful interiority of the protagonist seems to absorb whatever is around her. The surroundings are not merely exterior
symbols of a highly developed life of the intellect, they seem to be
part of it. Sémiramis is high up on a suspended bridge and she
sees far into the distance, a dominating and also far-reaching
mind. The air is as clear and transparent as her lucid intellect:
'De ces ponts suspendus, de ces ponts de roses, je jette de vastes
regards. Transparence de l'air et de ma pensée – choses qui se
conviennent les unes aux autres'.[7] Her awareness of the insig-
nificance of the antlike men she sees beneath her, the sense that
the city is nothing but a collection of objects to be manipulated,
is a direct communication of her enormous feelings of power:
'Ces fourmis sont à moi. Mon orgueil les dispose . . . Ces villes
sont des choses'. Surveying all of Babylon, she is drunk with
pride: 'Toute cette puissance, ces *perspectives* me *montent à la tête*.
Je respire de si haut, ces capiteuses altitudes et distances. Le
volume entier de ce monde. Ivresse de la grandeur. La vue a la
puissance de l'idée et du vin'. She breathes in the emanations of the
city and swells with pride and power: 'Tout mon empire est à

mes narines comme une évaporation infiniment pénétrante, qui fait ouvrir les poumons comme des *ailes intérieures*. Je respire mon pouvoir . . . Ma domination m'élève au ciel'. Is there not here an anticipation already of the protagonist of 'Le Cimetière Marin', for whom the sea is not merely an image of a powerful mind, but finally a living part of himself: 'O mon silence! . . . Edifice dans l'âme' (l. 17)?

LA JEUNE PARQUE

In early 1912, André Gide and Gaston Gallimard came to Valéry and attempted to persuade him to publish a collection of his early verse and prose. Valéry resisted the idea, although he was pre-occupied with his future and with what he would do after the death of Edouard Lebey, for whom he was working as a sort of secretary. Gallimard had a typescript prepared, and Valéry, weary of abstract thought, amused himself by making changes in his early poems, trying to improve musical continuity and to correct their unevenness. The old desire to write poetry, which he had never completely abandoned, grew stronger in him, and he began speculations on the problems poetry created in his mind. Speculation required in turn verification, and he started writing what he considered to be a final farewell poem to poetry which would run to some forty lines. In April 1917, after more than four years of work on some 800 pages of manuscript, this became the 512 lines of *La Jeune Parque*, one of the really great poems in French twentieth century literature. Writing it, Valéry had fortified his mind against the anguish of the war com-muniqués.

Valéry has emphasized that what interested him, as he turned seriously to poetry once again, was the degree of critical intelligence and will power he could exert in the creative process. It was an opportunity to use the scientific rigour, in which he had been training himself for twenty years, in something which would become a finished construction, a completed poem. In turn, this effort governed by *self-awareness* provided the poet with a constant series of illuminations on the functioning of the mind, and Valéry has affirmed that this was the greatest benefit he drew from four years of work. Valéry also placed in his poem the results of twenty years study of the living and functioning human being, modes of thinking and of feeling. He saw *La Jeune Parque* as a series of psychological states and said that the general subject of the poem was 'la Conscience de soi-même' (O.I, p. 1621), awareness of these states. But this intellectual surveillance, this awareness and curiosity in the Parque is always completed by imagery of the body. 'J'ai même été forcé, pour *attendrir* un peu le poème, d'y introduire des morceaux non prévus et faits après coup. Tout ce qui est sexuel est surajouté. Tel, le passage central sur le Printemps qui semble maintenant d'importance essentielle.' (O.I, p. 1621) This is no doubt an extreme statement, since at least part of the Serpent passage was written in 1913, and the lines: 'Quel repli de désirs, sa traîne! Quel désordre / De trésors s'arrachant à mon avidité' appear in the 'first state' of the poem, as well as the sexual 'soirée' passage:

> Souviens-toi de toi-même! O chaste joue, affronte
> L'innocente, coupable, et belle que je fus,
> Celle qui se fondant par les fluides fûts,
> Ennoblissait l'azur de la sainte distance!
> Ranime de ton sang la pâle circonstance,
> Le trouble transparent qui baigne dans les bois,
> Où tu te parlais seule, où j'écoutais ma voix
> Que j'ignorais si rauque et d'amour si voilée. . .
> Le col charmant cherchait la chasseresse ailée. . . [8]

It is likely, however, that the major theme of the poem unfolded for Valéry with the poem's development. That theme can perhaps best be described as a dramatic struggle between a desire for intellectual purity, for a god-like state, and the exigencies of life of a human being seen as a part of nature, and obeying inevitable laws of physiological functioning, development, reproduction and self-conservation.

Valéry, however, also affirmed that the content of the poem was made up of nothing but 'lieux communs' (O.I, p. 1622). This rather startling observation, as well as Valéry's revelation that the character of the poem appeared in its final stages, only serves to demonstrate that if one major aspect of poetic activity for Valéry was the exercise and discovery of his mind, the second was the achievement of the perfection of form. Telling how he began his poem, Valéry said: 'Je voyais quelque récitatif d'opéra à la Gluck; presque une seule phrase, longue, et pour contralto' (O.I, p. 1620). Still another well-known comment by the poet stresses the importance of continuity: *'La Jeune Parque* fut une recherche, littéralement indéfinie, de ce qu'on pourrait tenter en poésie qui fût analogue à ce qu'on nomme 'modulation' en musique. Les 'passages' m'ont donné beaucoup de mal. . .' (O.I, p. 1473). Wagner, as well as Gluck, inspired Valéry. The musical continuity of Racine's dramatic poetry was another model, particularly in such fragments as the 'songe d'Athalie' and the 'prière d'Esther'.[9] In 'Le Prince et la Jeune Parque' (O.I, pp. 1491–6), Valéry has told how an article of reminiscences in *Le Temps* of 1 December 1913 revealed to him precise details of the diction of the great tragedian Rachel (1812–58) in the part of Hermione in *Andromaque*, and how these details on her breathing, rhythm, accents, and the use of a voice which ranged over two octaves helped in a difficult moment of his work on *La Jeune Parque*.

Such an approach to poetry meant that Valéry was using words as a painter uses colours or a composer works with sounds, and in this attention to words, their musical and suggestive qualities, he carries on the tradition of the nineteenth century Symbolists while combining it with the strict rules of Classical prosody. A quotation from a notebook of 1914 proves how important words and formal considerations were in the creation of the content of the poem: 'Tout le développement (du Serpent) est sorti de la rime à *ordre*.'[10] Words, sounds, accents and rhythms are the substance of this poetry, as we can see so well in these two lines from Valéry's favourite passage:

> Pâle, qui se résigne et saigne sans regret?
> Que lui fait tout le sang qui n'est plus son secret?
>
> (ll. 387–8)

Who cannot be sensitive to the strong accent on 'Pâle', to the succession of slightly plaintive *i* sounds, to the soft music of the sibilants and the *gne* endings, as well as to the interplay of sound between *sans* and *sang* and the enriched rhyming words (*sans regret / son secret*)? While attentive to such details, Valéry also constantly interested himself in the formal structure of the whole poem. At one time he envisaged the 'Larme' and 'Suicide' sections as a conclusion to the poem. This was in the 'fourth state' of *La Jeune Parque*, which ran to 337 lines and was finished in May 1916, less than a year before publication. But finally these two sections were shifted to the end of the first part of the poem (ll. 280–324) while, as Duchesne-Guillemin has noted, other formal considerations created the conclusion.[11] Valéry confided to Emilie Noulet that he had to *finish* the poem, and it is likely that consideration of what would create a satisfying equilibrium with the previous passages devoted to reflections, death, night, sleep, defeat and regret weighed as heavily in the poet's mind as any intentions derived from his philosophy of life. Once again this implies that only through a study of its form can *La Jeune Parque* be truly appreciated.

Title, Epigraph, and Dedication. A number of possible titles were considered by Valéry as he wrote the poem before *La Jeune Parque* was decided on. These included: *Hélène, Larme, Pandore, Alpha de la Lyre, Ebauche, Etude Ancienne, Discours, La Seule Parque, l'Aurore, Ile,* and *Psyché.* The title *La Jeune Parque* was found early in 1916, at least a year before being finally selected. It suggests the idea of a 'young destiny', and like some of the other titles Valéry considered, it helps give a discreet colouration of antiquity to this poem written by a man born on the shores of the Mediterranean. Other allusions to antiquity appear in the reference to the Cygne-Dieu (l. 429), the image of the doves of Aphrodite (l. 186), the idea of the self or the world as a prison (l. 72, l. 331), and no doubt in the images of nudity and the occasional body-metaphor of the statue (l. 158). The epigraph ('Le Ciel a-t-il formé cet amas de merveilles / Pour la demeure d'un serpent?') comes from *Psyché* by Pierre Corneille, and contains an error. Corneille had written: 'Le Ciel aurait-il. . .' As Duchesne-Guillemin has pointed out, already the epigraph suggests an erotic metaphor, since the serpent in Corneille's play was nothing else than a disguise for Eros.[12] The dedication is to André Gide where Valéry refers to his poem as an 'exercice'. Once more he is emphasizing the formal considerations, the laws of prosody, the importance of will-power, effort, conscious awareness, critical alertness, and finally that benefit to which he gave such importance, the intellectual training obtained from four years of difficult work.

Lines 1–49. The poem begins with the Parque as a lone tragic figure in the vast grandiose scene of night sky, remote stars ('diamants extrêmes'), sea and rocky coast. Two poles: the remote heavens with their constellations, and the tormented intimacy of the self. The first two alexandrines are irregular, expressing by their rhythm the distress of the young girl. The broken rhythm is accompanied by sounds of lament, but this lament is neither declamatory nor lacking dignity. It is restrained and moving. Then in the third and the following lines, the Parque takes hold of herself, and the rhythm of the verses becomes regular.

The Parque now addresses her hand, pressed to her face and ready to console her, and which waits for a tear to fall and for an illumination of her broken heart. Once more the decor is evoked, now the sea (ll. 9–12) and it is particularly clear here how the decor will be used throughout the poem. At all times it will be intimately linked with the Parque herself. Here the sounds of the sea obviously reflect her own self-reproaching, disappointment and bitterness. In ll. 9 and 10, sibilants, the murmur of *me murmure*, and the dark vowels of *houle* and *ombre* make the presence of the sea very real, a sea already announced by the sibilant of *proche* in l. 3. Onomatopoetic effects, however, are very infrequent in Valéry's poetry, and usually the relation between sound and sense is more subtle, as in the acute vowels and nasals of ll. 10–12, expressive of the Parque's pain and lament.

Again in ll. 13–17, she turns to herself, to her cold hand and trembling breast, perhaps the first image in the poem which makes us powerfully aware of the physiological dimension of *La Jeune Parque*, an originality of which Valéry was particularly aware and justly proud. Line 13 in an early manuscript began with 'Que fais-je' which Valéry later altered to 'Que fais-tu', vastly improving the dramatic quality of the dialogue with the self. Then in ll. 14 and 15, we have the effective yet integrated metaphors, *feuille* and *îles*, for unlike the Surrealists of the 1920s, Valéry was intent on not breaking the continuity of the poem. In l. 16 the Parque begins turning toward the constellations above, with which she is *liée*, because they are symbols of purity, symbols of the Absolute, and soon she will tell how she turned toward the Absolute upon discovering that she was a mere mortal being. 'Soif de désastres' in l. 17 probably refers to her curiosity, to her desire to explore her painful duality, a need in her which constantly gives dynamism to the poem. The sky is *inconnu* (l. 16), because *she* has been changed by the powerful manifestation just now of her sexual nature.

Now the Parque begins an apostrophe to the pure and remote stars, in a discourse reminiscent of biblical style which once again elevates the tone of the poem. The Parque questions herself, seeking what caused her present pain. Was it because of a dream? The poem now moves into the very recent past in l. 32 as the Parque tells how she reacted to that dream, dominating her body, discovering its strange extent, strange because she had just awakened, but strange also, no doubt, because she was discovering its sexual nature. Then comes the famous l. 35 with its imagery of body, awareness of the body, and awareness of awareness: 'Je me voyais me voir. . .' In 1896, Monsieur Teste had already declared: 'Je suis étant, et me voyant; me voyant me voir, et ainsi de suite' (O.II, p. 25). The Parque gazed into the mysteries of her *profondes forêts* (l. 36), an image of the body and the world of the senses (cf. 'forêt sensuelle', l. 53 of 'Aurore' in *Charmes*). There her gaze followed the serpent who had just bitten her. There is a suggestion, of course, of the serpent in Genesis, but as Nadal has pointed out, the theological suggestions of *La Jeune Parque*, like the atmosphere of antiquity, are only superficial colourations.[13]

The serpent and its bite symbolize here the sexual nature of the Parque as well as her conscious awareness of herself, and not 'evil' or awareness of good and evil. She is 'sinueuse' (l. 35), because she contains this serpent within herself. In ll. 38–40, the rhythm of the verses reveals once again her emotion. She is aware not only of sexual feelings (*désirs, désordre, trésors*), but also of her dark thirst for clarity. 'Sombre' in l. 40 appears to be polyvalent, referring at the same time perhaps to the Parque's darkly mysterious inner life, her sexual nature, and her sorrow. Coiled around herself like a serpent, *she* is her 'seul possesseur' (l. 47), and within her a secret sister burns who prefers herself to that other part of the Parque which is 'extremely attentive'.

Lines 50–101. In a long passage, the Parque now quotes herself, repeating the words she used to dismiss the serpent, that 'orne-ment de ruine' (l. 54), 'bras de pierreries' (l. 58), who appears here again with emphasis on his sexual significance. The Parque is proud and strong, self-controlled, as her serpentine mind domi-nates herself ('je m'enlace' l. 51), and the passage is filled with imperatives. She explores her mind, realizes her limits (l. 68), although admitting that the weary mind can create illusions of power (ll. 69–72). Imagery of imprisonment and escape announce already passages evoking her ardour for the Absolute. Other inclinations can bring the return of the serpent, who now re-appears with imagery of caresses, languor and drunken passion. 'Thyrse' evokes the bacchantes, and this word again discreetly recalls classical antiquity. But once more she dismisses the serpent, and the alert, proud intellect triumphs. She emerges from an 'absence' (l. 92) (Valéry uses a word from Mallarmé's vocabulary), an absence whose mortal contours were soothed only by herself – and not by a lover. Duchesne-Guillemin raises a pertinent objection at this point in the poem, asserting that Valéry's method of working on separate fragments resulted occasionally in con-tradictions of sense: 'Mais alors, si elle vient d'avoir si bien conscience d'elle-même avant de commencer devant nous son chant, comment se fait-il que nous la voyions s'interroger et sembler à peine se réveiller?'[14] In ll. 97–101 which still evoke the Parque in the moments *preceding* ll. 1–27, she is lucid, aware of what has happened, and eager to preserve this new revelation about herself, this 'douleur divine' (l. 97), although the serpent has been dismissed. At the same time, this passage leads into an account of more distant memories, those of a 'mortelle sœur', a 'mensonge', an 'antique corps insensible'.

Lines 102–48. But this time of ignorance when she lived happily beneath the sun and by the sea was also a moment of unity of being and of union with the world. Valéry renews the image of the *chevelure.* Her flowing, wind-blown hair was no delight for men and lovers, but a symbol of freedom and of union with this seaside, sun-bathed decor. The rhythm is regular in the passage beginning with l. 110, reflecting the tranquillity and regularity of this life of pagan pleasures. It is one of the great sensual passages in Valéry's poetry with imagery of the soft pulp of blond flesh penetrated and devoured by the sun. In this distant past, however, she knew neither her sexual nature nor her eventual death, that 'amère saveur' (l. 117), which prolongs the fruit-image of l. 114. 'Captive' (l. 122) with its seventeenth century suggestion (*captive par amour*), she strode through banks of flowers which were bent over by a simple and virginal dress discreetly apparent on the 'vivantes couleurs' (l. 131) of her nude body. Valéry is far from the ornamented women of Baudelaire.

The Parque half regrets those innocent happy days of the harmonious self when there was no hesitation between wish and action. Everything seemed unchanging and eternal until one day when watching her shadow glide over the earth, she realized that she was mortal and that she would finally die. Acute *i* sounds accent the anxiety of this realization in ll. 141–2 and again in 145–8.

Lines 148–221. She was 'captive' (l. 156) then of the perfume of orange flowers (l. 151), and the evaporation of these perfumes symbolizes the passing of all things and time. She lost interest in her surroundings, and if her body trembled beneath the sun's rays, it had become a statue (l. 158), no longer 'Poreuse' (l. 113). Then once again she passes to present time in ll. 153–5, as she penetrates deeper into the mysteries of the self beneath the night sky. Her eye, dark with astonishment, contemplated her desire for death (l. 161), and from the beginning of the passage she was 'armed' (l. 149) by the idea of death. Her response to mortality was a death chosen by her, and in ll. 165–6 she thinks of the death-wish of the Pythia, and acute vowels again appear in the verses. (There is an allusion here no doubt to Valéry's 'La Pythie' in *Charmes.*) Then in l. 170 she watched a bird in the sky, its 'miroir d'aile' (constructed from 'miroir aux alouettes') and saw it disappear and die in the dark gaze of her eye.

Line 173 is elliptical, and 'j'étais' should be understood after the word 'regard'. It was dangerous (for her) to be the prey of her eye with its dreams of death, because that eye, from its soft lids ('plages de soie'), l. 174, had already seen too many identical days. Because she knew she would die, life lost its savour and nothing had value any more (l. 179). Thus she was no longer existing in time, but was half-dead, or half-immortal (ll. 180–1), and her future history was 'cold', without interest, and the self detached ('feux absolus') from any participation in life. Will Time dare from various past days ('diverses tombes') l. 185, recall an evening favoured by the doves of Aphrodite? (cf. 'Episode' in *Album de Vers Anciens*, O.I, p. 83). This evening brings with it a blush of shame attached to this fragment ('lambeau voyageur') of her childhood, and mixes a rose colour with the emerald tones of sunset.

Now the Parque tells how on this particular evening she experienced her first sexual feelings, which she recognizes now, but did not recognize then. She asks her memory to bring a blush to her face as a sign of refusal of that other self (ll. 190–2). Then she orders her blood to give life to the remote memory ('pâle circonstance') and to the innocent self of the old happy days (l. 195). Finally that blood will be a fire consuming the pale memory (l. 196). She wants to recognize and hate that child and 'ce silence complice', and in this phrase the sounds become soft and caressing. Let her voice cry out again, with its cry of love, love she had not recognized because she was seeking *death*: 'Le col charmant cherchant la chasseresse ailée' (l. 202). The image suggests a swan's neck and the swan's legendary song at the moment of death, while 'la chasseresse' is a winged arrow and no doubt also Artemis, 'a huntress and a "lion unto women"', because their sudden and painless deaths are ascribed to her' (*Oxford Classical Dictionary*). Vines brushed her cheek, 'grands cils', lashes of an imagined lover, and the light of evening was criss-crossed with lashes and fluid tree-trunks communicating a sense of confusion, disorder and movement created by the powerful sexual desires of the Parque. The hypallages of l. 208 suggest that it was she who was 'broken' and 'confused'.

In l. 209 she again quotes words she spoke in the past. The ardour she didn't recognize at the time as a sexual reaction was an élan toward death – not an ordinary accidental or normal one, but a chosen death which she saw as the attainment of an absolute, immortality, a divine state. Her eyes would be like stars (cf. ll. 18–23) tracing the *templum* (Latin: space marked out by the augur's baton) in the sky, while her body would become the object of a cult. The imperfect tense of l. 211 glides into the present tense of l. 212 as the Parque is again seized by desire for death. Vertigo confuses her vision and piercing *i* sounds reappear beginning with l. 213. She implores death to deliver her, and the Platonic theme of man as slave or prisoner of the body (cf. ll. 331, 482) occurs in ll. 219–20. Then with a skilful modulation through the rhyme, we pass to the famous 'springtime' passage in l. 222, originally a separate poem, 'Renaissance', and added in the final stages of the writing of *La Jeune Parque*.

Lines 222–372. The originality of the magnificent 'springtime' passage, so forceful and lyrical, lies in its attention to the real elements and actions of springtime rather than in simply the feelings of the poet:

> Demain, sur un soupir des Bontés constellées,
> Le printemps vient briser les fontaines scellées:
> L'étonnant printemps rit, viole . . . On ne sait d'où
> Venu? Mais la candeur ruisselle à mots si doux
> Qu'une tendresse prend la terre à ses entrailles. . .
>
> (ll. 225–9)

Just as it is the blood of the Parque which is affected by the coming of spring, we have the action of the winds, the breaking-up of ice, the flowing of water, sap rising in the trunks, and leaves bursting out on the branches. The physiology of springtime is linked with the physiology of the Parque. 'Bontés constellées' in l. 225 are the winds and stars of spring. 'Etonnant' in l. 227 should be understood in its old sense of 'provoking a strong reaction', 'Ecailles' in l. 230 are the leaves of the trees, and in l. 238 'ramer' is a play-on-words implying both 'rames' and 'rameaux'. According to Lucienne Cain, ll. 230–2 were written in 1897![15]

The Parque herself experiences a powerful sexual response to this arrival of springtime, asking with a pathetic repetition of 'Quelle' (l. 243), who could resist such an appeal? Sighs lift her breasts (l. 248) (cf. 'L'Abeille' in *Charmes* for the same rhyme abeille / corbeille), and the image of the bee (l. 250), always linked with the mind in both *La Jeune Parque* and *Charmes*, signifies a critical moment of choice between the 'Lumière' (l. 253) of life, or death and purity. Typical physiological imagery is continued in ll. 254–5 where we sense the beating of her heart, and where her breast, captive of its network of veins, burns and swells. Then in

l. 257 the theme of sexual response shifts to the theme of maternity. Again the image of the 'autel' recurs (cf. l. 210) with its discreet coloration of Antiquity, but here the Parque would be sacrificed to life and its cycles, 'éternels retours' (l. 263). Furthermore, giving life implies another eventual death like the one she discovered (ll. 141–8). She cries out her refusal in an exclamatory passage (l. 269), where Valéry uses a series of negatives and substantives, a rhetorical device unusual in his poetry: 'Non, souffles! Non, regards, tendresses . . . mes convives.' The passage ends with a concern for others (l. 278), surprising in this poem centred on the Parque.

Then this pity for others becomes an admission of her own defeat, in an extraordinary physiological passage which traces the progress of tears along their paths from secret inner grottos until they obscure her vision. 'Envieuse' in l. 281 is an archaism meaning 'desirous'. 'Orgueil' in l. 285 refers to the tear itself, proud product of this labyrinth and now forced outward: 'contrainte', (l. 286). 'Sacrifier' and 'libation' (ll. 288–9) again suggest Antiquity. Then the theme of tears modulates into the theme of suicide as the Parque wanders closer to the precipice overlooking the sea. 'Cygne' in l. 307 is an image of her own body, rather than some prospective lover (cf. 'col charmant' l. 202). Her 'pact' (l. 311) with the earth implies that she too is earth. At the end of the passage, however, she hesitates. 'Celui' should be understood before 'qui' in l. 322, and l. 324, although repeating l. 304, indicates that she is turning back from the edge of the cliff.

Lines 325–60. Between l. 324 and l. 325 the Parque again sleeps and then re-awakens as dawn appears. Valéry himself said: 'Je vois, par exemple, un commencement d'*acte* à ce vers' (O.I, p. 1626). The apostrophe to herself, 'Mystérieuse MOI' (l. 325) is intended, of course, to recall another apostrophe, 'Harmonieuse MOI' (l. 102), communicating to the reader their contrast as well as a sense of all that has occurred between the two moments in the poem. There is a significant contrast also between the black night and heaving sea of ll. 316–21 and the bright dawn and calm sea of this new episode, but for the Parque nothing seems changed. The sun ('un miroir', l. 327) rises from the sea, the stars ('signes', l. 329) fade away, but the Parque is still the same, still a prisoner of life (l. 331), 'victime inachevée' (l. 335), 'impérissable hostie' (l. 338), (again allusions to Antiquity). The calm waves wash her body ('seuil', 'écueil', ll. 335–6), but it is a body ready to turn again to desires and tormented by memories. Then this theme of sameness and ennui modulates to one of renewal, purity and laughter, radically changing 'la tombe enthousiaste' (l. 346), that burial place where her élan towards death was a divinely inspired frenzy. Now she eagerly greets the islands, not yet visible, and this image recalls that 'Ile' was once considered as a title for the poem, symbol of the isolated inner drama of the Parque. Here they are 'jouets de la jeune lumière' (l. 349), and the expression suggests childhood, gaiety, activity. Soon they will be beehives of action (ll. 350–5), and the image resembles a stanza of 'Air de Sémiramis':

> Soleil, soleil, regarde en toi rire mes ruches!
> L'intense et sans repos Babylone bruit,
> Toute rumeurs de chars, clairons, chaînes de cruches
> Et plaintes de la pierre au mortel qui construit.
>
> (O.I, p. 93)

Finally, the Parque calls the islands 'merveilleuses Parques', because they are like human destinies, participating in life, creating flowers in the air, but in the depths of the sea cold and dead.

Lines 361–80. The word 'glacés' (l. 360) brings back thoughts of death, and the Parque recounts recent memories now, nocturnal memories evoked in daylight, whereas the first part of the poem contained daylight memories recounted at night. Moreover, the second part is far more an account, and even at times an account of what *might* have been, while the first part had a larger proportion of lines devoted to present action. Beginning with l. 361, the Parque tells what happened in the hours between l. 324 and l. 325. She left the precipice and went back home, in a calmer state, still, however, seeking death and listening to the final beats of her heart (again a physiological detail). But with an image which recalls Mallarmé's Hérodiade looking into her mirror (l. 380), she realizes that she had experienced no real movement toward death.

Lines 381–405. Valéry wrote of this passage of *La Jeune Parque*: 'De ces morceaux, il en est un qui, seul, représente pour moi le poème que j'aurais voulu faire. Ce sont les quelques vers qui commencent ainsi: "*O n'aurait-il fallu, folle,* etc." ' (O.I, p. 1621). It is a dynamic, suggestive passage culminating in a magnificent image of the rising, expanding smoke of a funeral pyre mingling with the constellations in the heavens, but despite its emotional moments, the whole passage has an extraordinary continuity. In the opening lines, the Parque regrets her last chance for a proud refusal of life, a 'transparente mort' (l. 384) identified with purity. Beginning with l. 386, the third person is used to evoke a powerful vision of what might have been. Then ll. 395–6 are slowed by punctuation as she begins to identify with the vision, and the first person is used again. After this, in the concluding third of the passage, the verses become more rapid and emphatic. The rhyme *fumée/consumée* significantly recalls the fifth stanza of 'Le Cimetière Marin', and the word 's'abandonne' in l. 402 recalls l. 34 of the same poem: 'Je m'abandonne à ce brillant espace'. Dentals accent the expansion of l. 402, and there is a shift to the present tense recalling the movement in ll. 211–12, as her 'essence' mingles with the stars.

Lines 406–64. But in l. 406, the Parque stops short, and refuses to undergo again the élan toward death of ll. 211–17. 'Sombre lys', 'dark allusion' (cf. 'Le Cimetière Marin', ll. 42, 47), she couldn't conquer the desire of the body to *live*, and always curious, always searching within herself, she seeks to discover that thread of instinct (an allusion to Theseus and Ariadne) which brought her back to life and the new day. The image of the serpent recurs in l. 423, interestingly polyvalent, called forth by the sensuality of the perfumed breast, the idea of a sinuous return to life, and finally by the dark and sad animality of l. 424 which perhaps borrows from an image of Rimbaud's 'Le Bateau Ivre':

> Echouages hideux au fond des golfes bruns
> Où les serpents géants dévorés des punaises
> Choient, des arbres tordus, avec de noirs parfums!
>
> (ll. 54–6)

She was betrayed by the 'chair profonde' (l. 425) and the nasal suggests the deep mysteries of the flesh. But there was no sexual dream – the first of several allusions to the beginning of the poem – she simply fell asleep. Several details remind us of the seaside decor, 'conque' (l. 440) and 'reflux' (l. 441). Sorensen has commented on the moving simplicity of the comparison (rarely used by Valéry in *La Jeune Parque*) with the bird alighting in order to rest.[16] She descends to a sort of death, commanded by mysteriously dominating shades, and she is a victim offered to the night, 'bras suppliciés' (l. 455), cf. 'mains abandonnées' (l. 449). She returns to 'le germe', to the original and fertile beginning of beings, and to a 'sombre innocence' (l. 458) which calls forth again the image of the serpent and the word 'trésors' (cf. l. 39). Then this magnificent 'physiological' passage closes with a seemingly endless alexandrine, slowed by six accents, and the only remaining italicized lines of the poem, a passage of pure Surrealism:

> (*La porte basse c'est une bague . . . où la gaze
> Passe . . . Tout meurt, tout rit dans la gorge qui jase . . .
> L'oiseau boit sur ta bouche et tu ne peux le voir . . .
> Viens plus bas, parle bas . . . Le noir n'est pas si noir. . .*)
> (ll. 461–4)

Lines 465–512. All her pride was mingled with lowly dreams, uncontrolled by the highest faculties of the intellect, when her body spread itself upon the bed, freeing her in sleep: 'lasse femme absolue' (l. 477). It is a sleep like death, a mystical fusion with the universe (l. 469), but it is not the exalted death of ll. 395–405. The mysterious ark of the body (l. 481), its contours and charms (l. 478), and desire for love (l. 479), prevented her suicide, and her violent emotions became nothing more than lamentations.

The 'jeune soleil' (l. 487), and the adjective is an hypallage here, suggesting not only the freshness of morning, but also the youth and vigour of the Parque, sweeps away remorse, and the young girl watches without emotion the disappearance of the star of inhuman purity (l. 486). She offers herself once more to the sun, recalling the imagery of ll. 107–14, but the image is an ambiguous one in both passages. If in ll. 107–14 she was innocent, yet already unconsciously yielding to sexual inclinations, here at the end of the poem she is offering herself to more than a mere sexual destiny. This superb ending is an eager acceptance by the

Parque, and by Valéry himself, of the totality of life and all its possibilities:

Le pas le plus difficile que l'homme aura à franchir, si son développement se poursuit, sera l'acceptation—et surtout l'accoutumance à—ou *l'assimilation de l'acceptation* de la 'vie' telle quelle – sans illusions.

Ressentir, en somme, comme naturel ce qui est naturel.

Ne pas demander une vie éternelle — comme un enfant demande la lune. (*Cahiers* II, pp. 1439–40)

The powerful, brilliant finale, after an initial question, occupies a long period of seventeen lines. As in the first lines of the poem, the Parque again approaches the sea, but here her body is no longer filled with a weak trembling. It is thoroughly alive, roused by a sharp awakening, and the bitter, reproachful sea of l. 11 is now a 'riante amertume' (l. 498). The whole ending is filled with imagery of vivacity and expansion. The wind, 'âme intense' (l. 501), whips the waves, destroying a monster of purity (l. 503). 'Une vierge de sang' (l. 511), a living virgin with golden breasts, lifts herself in sacrifice toward the rising sun (cf. l. 118). The affirmation of the final line is powerfully reinforced by a bold borrowing from Catholic ritual: ('sous les espèces du pain et du vin').

CHARMES

Valéry published *Charmes*, a collection of twenty-two poems, some elaborated while he was still composing *La Jeune Parque*, on 25 June 1922. These are suggestive poems, ambiguous, sometimes mysterious, giving the impression of being closely attached to the poet himself, of reflecting his deepest concerns, his *vie intérieure*. Their musicality is a realization of the æsthetic objective of Valéry's youth and the Symbolist poetry of the late nineteenth century. An unbroken continuity of beautiful sounds creates that enchantment, that 'charm', that magic spell, that superior removal from ordinary existence which for Valéry was the object of poetry. This is 'poésie pure', or at least an approximation of it, a poetry far from *la vie quotidienne*, from banal emotions, from personal confessions, from the common use of words, from prose. It is essentially a poetry of language, both personal and universal, incantatory, polyvalent, sensual, physiological, sometimes witty, sometimes exalted, sometimes intimate and tender. A poetry of language implies preoccupation with form, and it is the great variety of forms which first strikes the reader of *Charmes*: odes, elegies, a quatorzain, one regular and irregular sonnets, lines of 5, 6, 7, 8, 10 and 12 syllables. Valéry has described the formal origins of 'Le Cimetière Marin' and 'La Pythie' (O.I, p. 1503 and O.I, p. 1338-9). Formal considerations governed the elaboration of all these poems, economy of language, harmony of sound, relations of words to each other, and also the architecture of the entire poem. The 'Zeno' stanza of 'Le Cimetière Marin' (ll. 121-6) introduces a philosophical colouration to counter the emotional intensity of preceding stanzas. In 'La Fausse Morte', 'La Dormeuse' and 'L'Abeille,' there is a careful balancing of *préciosité* and sensuality. Yet every poem of *Charmes* unfolds according to an unexpected development, and Valéry liked to vary the point of view in the sonnet, as in 'Le Sylphe', or to vary the tones of stanzas, as in 'Ebauche d'un Serpent'. Still, although he sought variety and the unexpected, he was careful to preserve perfect continuity and to create interrelationships between various parts of the poem.

Thus, throughout 'Le Sylphe' acute sounds dominate and they help to create a rapid rhythm in the five syllable lines reflecting the alertness of the intellect in its various attitudes. In the quatrains a fleeting and unexpected inspiration arrives magically, 'ni vu ni connu', in the poet's mind, and he must seize it before it disappears. The refrain is then varied in the first tercet, wittily mocking readers and critics who fail to understand Valéry's poetry. Then in the final stanza the refrain of the quatrains returns to evoke the magical appearance of an image, a woman's breast, and its dazzling, instantaneous effect. 'C'est un grand avantage pour un poète que l'incapacité où la plupart des êtres se sentent de pousser leur pensée *au delà* du point où elle éblouit, excite, transporte. L'étincelle illumine un lieu qui semble infini au petit temps donné pour le voir. L'expression éblouit' (O.I, p. 395).

Again in 'La Pythie', Valéry is showing mental functionings not initially controlled by the conscious mind of the poet, here the irrational and powerful forces of the sensibility, emotions which can be dangerous but also creative, and thus this long

poem begins with animal terms for a crazed priestess but ends with:
'Honneur des Hommes, SAINT LANGAGE' when enthusiasm
is finally chained in impersonal, beautiful language. 'La Pythie'
was the result of a challenge from Valéry's friend Pierre Louÿs
who reproached him with failing to exploit the octosyllabic metre,
one of the most important in French poetry. Valéry composed the
poem in twenty-three ten-line stanzas, a form borrowed from
Victor Hugo, brilliantly varying the tone and imagery of the
stanzas to reflect the changing moods.

'Palme' is a third poem concerned with unconscious forces of
the mind. Here the poet struggles with his poem, and nothing
seems to happen, no progress is made. But while the poet feels
helpless and frustrated, something is going on, a poem is
slowly being formed in a hidden part of the mind which secretly
collaborates with the desires and orientation of the conscious
intellect. 'Palme' is a poem of calm, and patience, and waiting,
but also of constant, although mysterious intellectual functioning
and ultimate triumph. Valéry has used the same ten-line heptasyllabic stanza as in 'Aurore', with which 'Palme' was once
joined. The length of the stanzas gives a sense of each stage of the
slow ripening of a poem while the short seven-syllable line is
well-adapted to an impression of secret movement. But the lines
are slower here than 'Aurore', a poem of self-confident and rapid
production. One should compare the first stanza of 'Palme' with
its weaker verbs, broad *a* sounds, and more frequent pauses with
the beginning of 'Aurore'. Both poems, however, have the same
powerfully sensual fruit images to evoke poetry, demonstrating
once again the role of sensibility, and even sensuality, in Valéry's
poetry. The fruits here grow, of course, on a palm tree, rising
alone in the desert and symbolizing the solitary poet and his
empty, seemingly unproductive days: 'Ces jours qui te semblent
vides' (l. 61). Trees are a favourite image in Valéry's poetry, and
they appear prominently in *La Jeune Parque*, in 'Au Platane' and
'Ebauche d'un Serpent.' The tree image in 'Palme' emphasizes
that poetry comes from deep within the mind and body, and not
from the visions of a *voyant*. The roots of the tree plunge into the
earth in search of water, and slowly the sap rises in the trunk and
ripens the fruit on the branches.

'Aurore' gives a very different view of what writing poetry

can be like. Here the poet seems almost overwhelmed by an abundance of inspiration and so the operation of the conscious mind is far more apparent, with an exercise of will-power signified by a repetition of 'Je' throughout the poem. 'Aurore' is an 'intellectual promenade' undertaken in those very early morning hours favoured by Valéry. Emerging from sleep he strides confidently through a garden of the mind where he first sights 'Similitudes amies / Qui brillez parmi les mots!' (ll. 13–14), harmonies between words. But as he starts up the ladder to gather in these fruits, he notices waking women who are his 'Idées', favourite enigmas, with whom he engages in alert and witty dialogue. Then with the sixth stanza he leaves the ideas and turns instead to the 'forêt sensuelle' of sensibility and poetry. The ten-line stanza form is perfectly adapted to an evocation of each stage of this intellectual journey. The heptasyllabic line, now quicker than in 'Palme', suggests that nothing resists the will of this active, vigorous mind. Even so, there are suggestions of hesitancy in ll. 59 and 74, of waiting in l. 70, of difficulties in stanza eight. If the will is prominent here, poetic inspiration still originates, as in 'Palme', from the depths of the mysterious sensibility, from the 'forêt sensuelle' (l. 53), the 'vignes ombreuses' (l. 61), and in the last, almost visionary stanza, from 'la profondeur infinie' of a pool where a swan-like young girl swims, allegory of hope and of the birth of form.

Again in 'Poésie' a rapid heptasyllabic line and brief four-line stanzas communicate the excitement of plenitude of poetic inspiration, and again the sensuality of Valéry's poetry is stressed, here through the allegory of a nursing mother and child accompanied by that of a lover and mistress. Both allegories are brought to life with sensations and emotions and even mystical exaltation. The flow of inspiration has suddenly been stopped, however, and it is on this deprivation that the poem focusses in the beginning and closing stanzas. The mind has passed judgement, no longer accepting the inspiration pouring forth:

> O rigueur, tu m'es un signe
> Qu'à mon âme je déplus!'
> (ll. 29–30)

'Le Cantique des Colonnes' is the last of the poems devoted to

the important theme of the creation of art, and again, as in
'Poésie' there is a four-line stanza with alert brief verses, here six-
syllable lines, again communicating the vivacity of the intellect,
but here that of the spectator who gazes on a temple and is
stimulated in many varied ways. Unlike the five preceding poems,
'Le Cantique des Colonnes' emphasizes only the calculating
conscious mind in the act of creation, although emotions and
even a discreet sensuality are present in the reactions of the viewer
to whom these columns appear as young girls. Thus the poem
anticipates Eupalinos who built a temple which was 'l'image
mathématique d'une fille de Corinthe que j'ai heureusement
aimée' (O.II, p. 92). The stress in 'Le Cantique des Colonnes' is
on conscious calculation in the creative act rather than on
'inspiration', perhaps because Valéry is emphasizing here the
theme of 'formal arts', music and architecture. For Valéry the
formal arts were more amenable to calculation, rigour, and true
composition, and this is why the sensual beauty of the columns
seems to emerge only from laws and numbers:

> Nos antiques jeunesses,
> Chair mate et belles ombres,
> Sont fières des finesses
> Qui naissent par les nombres!
>
> Filles des nombres d'or,
> Fortes des lois du ciel,
> Sur nous tombe et s'endort
> Un dieu couleur de miel.
>   (ll. 45-52)

'Le Cantique des Colonnes', with its emphasis on mental
rigour, shows that no hard and fast line can be drawn between
the poems of *Charmes* presenting artistic creation and those
devoted to 'thinking', and of course Valéry himself, as he made
clear in the 'Introduction à la Méthode de Léonard de Vinci' in
1894, did not separate these two functions of the mind. 'L'Abeille',
'Les Grenades' and 'Ode Secrète' could be poems about the
writing of poetry. This theme, however, is not specifically present
in these poems and so they can be seen in a more general way as
poems about the functioning of the mind. In the irregular sonnet
'L'Abeille', a drowsy mind seeks the stimulation of thought. As

often in Valéry's poetry, the imagery is sexual, although a pro-
nounced *préciosité* suggests that this sexuality is allegorical.
Assonanced feminine rhymes in the quatrains create an impression
of monotonous languor, while the exclusively masculine rhymes
of the tercets reflect the longed-for activity.

'Les Grenades' also begins with slow octosyllabic lines which
then become more rapid, contriving to suggest the long and
slow maturing of thought, which finally bursts forth in the alert
brief words of the first tercet. Hard sounds predominate because
this is a poem about intellectual force. The spirit of Monsieur
Teste inhabits 'Les Grenades' and also 'Ode Secrète' which sings
of the secret triumph of an intellectual hero who struggles, con-
quers and then rests. The pattern of imagery in 'Ode Secrète,
follows an order opposite to that of 'L'Abeille' where the immobility of fatigue evolved toward the mobility of thought. In
'Ode Secrète' the movement and order of the dance, symbol of
thinking, gives way to the immobility and disorder of sleep:

> Ce grand corps qui fit tant de choses,
> Qui dansait, qui rompit Hercule,
> N'est plus qu'une masse de roses!
>
> (ll. 10–12)

As the thinker sleeps, the imagery of mobility and order is taken
over by constellations in the night sky, symbols of human triumph:

> Dormez, sous les pas sidéraux,
> Vainqueur lentement désuni,
> Car l'Hydre inhérente au héros
> S'est éployée à l'infini. . .
>
> (ll. 13–16)

Another group of poems, 'Ebauche d'un Serpent', 'L'Insinuant', 'Le Cimetière Marin', 'Fragments du Narcisse', 'Au
Platane' and 'Le Rameur', consider thought from a more general
and philosophical point of view and are among the most important
poems of *Charmes*. The theme of 'Ebauche d'un Serpent' is the
intellectual independence of man which ends by discovering the
imperfections of life, its traps and torments, such as death,
specifically mentioned in lines 22 and 299. But this brilliant
poem also sings a magnificent hymn to the tree of knowledge and

the ending is triumphant. Furthermore, Valéry defends himself against the seductive Serpent with a witty burlesque treatment of his role. The Serpent is boastful, arrogant, even vulgar, and Valéry exaggerated alliteration to further the burlesque effect:

> Ce lieu charmant qui vit la chair
> Choir et se joindre m'est très cher!
>
> (ll. 45-6)

The poem is remarkable for its technical virtuosity, the great variety of rhyme schemes and the changes of tone from stanza to stanza which, according to Valéry, gave him great difficulty. It is perhaps for these aspects that James Joyce preferred this poem to all the others in *Charmes*. Typically, Valéry regretted its inclusion in the volume. 'Ebauche d'un Serpent', as its title indicates, was only the first version of the poem he would have liked to write, and the little poem 'L'Insinuant' can be considered another version of the subject of the temptation of thought, but in a radically different form: four four-line stanzas of five syllable verse. The brevity of the lines gives importance to the rhyming words, restricts the poet to only minimal use of visual imagery, and excludes entirely the elaborate argumentation of the 310-line 'Ebauche'. In 'L'Insinuant', Valéry suggests instead a sequence of attitudes: a seductive, self-admiring serpent in the first stanza becomes assured and insinuating in the second, patient and voluptuous in the fourth, opposite a smiling but hesitant Eve, who appears only in the third stanza.

The death-theme of 'Ebauche d'un Serpent' has even more prominence in 'Le Cimetière Marin.' This poem and 'Fragments du Narcisse' communicate the failure of 'self-possession', of perfect knowledge and control of the self. 'Le Cimetière Marin' is Valéry's best-known poem, more accessible than the greater *La Jeune Parque*, and it has been translated into many languages. The last two lines of the first stanza are engraved on Valéry's tomb in the cemetery by the sea in Sète, where the poet was born in 1871 and where he was buried in 1945. The poem explores the two tragic themes of the impossibility of intellectual self-possession in life and the disappearance of individual existence in death, and thus its epigraph, from Pindar, announces: 'Do not aspire to any eternal or infinite life, but exhaust what you can accomplish in reality.' It is well-known that the poem had a purely formal origin, in a decasyllabic rhythm empty of words which came to Valéry's mind one day. Typically, he saw the rhythm as a challenge, and undertook to give the ten-syllable line the strength of an alexandrine by using mostly lines with a 4/6 division, and also by increasing the number of effective words. The poem is even more richly rhymed than *La Jeune Parque*, 'Fragments du Narcisse', and 'Ebauche d'un Serpent', and its great incantatory stanzas, such as the first, or the tenth, and the lines of its exultant conclusion, which affirms the possibilities of life, remain in the minds of readers of French poetry the world over.

The death-theme appears still again in 'Fragments du Narcisse', in the concluding lines of the third section of the poem. This poem, which expresses the futile search of self in sensual and even sexual imagery, is even more accessible than 'Le Cimetière Marin'. Valéry himself said that his intention was to write a poem far simpler in form and meaning than *La Jeune Parque* and that his major effort was directed toward the creation of harmonious sound.

The theme of Narcissus first appears in Valéry's poetry with a sonnet in September 1890, and is continued in the 53 lines of 'Narcisse Parle', published in *La Conque* in March 1891, and later, in revised form, in the *Album de Vers Anciens* in 1920. The first section of 'Fragments du Narcisse' appeared in the first edition of *Charmes*, in 1922,[17] but with a Narcissus quite different from the languishing hero of 'Narcisse Parle'. In *Charmes* he is a vigorous, forceful protagonist, and his emotions and desires give energy to each image. Part II and III appeared in the February 1926 edition of *Charmes*, and the first section of the second part reflects no doubt the end of Valéry's brief but momentous love affair with Catherine Pozzi in passages rivalling the Hugo of 'Tristesse d'Olympio'.

Like 'Fragments du Narcisse' and 'Le Cimetière Marin', 'Au Platane' and 'Le Rameur' also take a philosophical attitude toward intellectual activity. Valéry was haunted by the need to liberate his mind from everything, to detach it from anything impeding pure intellectual functioning, from such things as habits, opinions, emotional preferences. It is impressive to see how important this theme is in the daily private notes of his *Cahiers*. It is an attitude which is a major key to understanding Valéry. The theme is prominent already in 'La Soirée avec Monsieur Teste' and it dominates a poem in *Charmes* where the tree-image is again important, as it was in 'Ebauche d'un Serpent'. In 'Au Platane' the immobile tree, rooted in the ground, symbolizes man, or the thinker, inevitably limited by the fact that he is born in a certain place and at a certain time and can never entirely liberate himself from his own existence. Duchesne-Guillemin has commented on the traditional stanza of this beautiful elegy, remarking that the brief six-syllable line always following the lengthy alexandrine recalls man to his limited condition.[18] The imagery and spirit of the poem are by no means entirely negative, however. Part of the poem presents a typical Valerian sexual image of nature in a sensual vision of trees imagined as young women, while opposed to this image there is characteristic Valerian dynamism in the forceful vitality of the heroic plane tree pushing upward toward the sky, and a typical contrast of ordered thought with the 'confuse cendre' from which the tree emerges. Significant oppositions of order and disorder appear also in 'Ode Secrète', 'Ebauche d'un Serpent', 'Le Vin Perdu' and elsewhere.

'Le Rameur' again presents limits impeding the mind of the thinker. A man is rowing upstream on a river with great effort, passing beneath a succession of bridges. It is clear that the river suggests time, the duration of a man's life, and its banks and direction imply that this life has inevitably progressed along one path, according to certain choices which necessarily excluded others. The heavy stone bridges are undoubtedly successive prisons of the self; the symbol is similar to the 'citerne' in stanza 8 of 'Le Cimetière Marin' and to the tomb-image of line 72 of *La Jeune Parque*. The rower is trying to nullify the effects of time, trying to break free of these prisons as he moves upstream toward that 'pureté du non-être' longed for in l. 30 of 'Ebauche d'un Serpent': 'Je remonte à la source où cesse même un nom' (l. 16). Once more we have a characteristic Valerian poem of will-power and dynamism. The heavy alexandrines of the four-line stanzas suggest with their strong cesuras a regularity of movement and of effort:

Penché contre un grand fleuve, infiniment mes rames
M'arrachent à regret aux riants environs;
Ame aux pesantes mains, pleines des avirons,
Il faut que le ciel cède au glas des lentes lames.

(ll. 1-4)

The theme of women in Valéry's poetry is also related to that
ideal freedom of the mind which dominates 'Au Platane' and 'Le
Rameur'. Significantly, there are no 'love poems' in *Charmes* and
it is significant too that women are only discreetly present in the
four short poems where they play a role in the life of the poet.[19]
The woman in 'La Dormeuse' may be 'ma jeune amie', but she is
asleep, and the poet looks on her as a spectator, and one who
cannot penetrate the secrets of her dreams. She becomes pro-
gressively more remote, first 'amie', then 'femme endormie',
'ennemie', 'La Dormeuse', and finally 'amas'. Here, however, a
turning-point is reached, a contact is made with the naked sleeping woman, although only an æsthetic contact, even if sensual and
tender: 'ta forme veille, et mes yeux sont ouverts.' This is the only
regular sonnet in *Charmes* and the only sonnet written in alexandrines, long verses so well-suited to the calm and heaviness of
sleep in the quatrains and to the sensuality of the sleeping nude in
the tercets.

'La Fausse Morte', a poem of mixed alexandrines and octosyllabic lines, offers an image of love-making, but still the woman
is hardly present, except, significantly, when she wakes suddenly
from 'death' and takes the initiative of violence. There is a
charming sensuality, even a tenderness, in the slow murmuring
alexandrines of the first stanza, prolonged by echoing octosyllabic
lines. The poem, however, ends in the second stanza with a
sudden transformation of languor into vivacity and the precious
wit of a concluding triple paradox which disengages the protagonist from sexual charms. In a similar manner, 'Intérieur'
begins with slow and sensual alexandrines and the muted presence
of a woman moving about the room. But this woman's eyes never
meet those of the thinker seated in this room, and if a certain
sensuality hovers over the poem, it does not seem to endanger the
intellect:

Elle met une femme au milieu de ces murs
Qui, dans ma rêverie errant avec décence,
Passe entre mes regards sans briser leur absence,

(ll. 4–6)

'Les Pas' is certainly the most tender of these poems, yet even here the image of the woman is attenuated. A succession of octosyllabic quatrains conveys the even movement of a woman toward the bed of the waiting thinker who speaks of her approach with exalted language. She is, however, a phantom-like figure, a divinity, and if the exalted language seems tender, it also creates the same distance between poet and woman which was evident in 'La Dormeuse', 'La Fausse Morte' and 'Intérieur'. She is there to bring a consoling kiss to this weary thinker; the poem, however, does not end in union but with the poet's plea to the woman to wait while he savours the moment. There is a shift at the end from the intimate form of address to the respectful 'vous'. This is the closest Valéry comes to a love-poem in *Charmes*.

Sexual imagery plays a role also in 'La Ceinture', but in the form of a sexual vision of the day's end, just as the trees of 'Au Platane' were transformed into ardent young women. 'La fin du jour est femme', Valéry once wrote as an aphorism (O.I, p. 303). The end of the day is also, however, death, and Valéry subtly mingles the two themes in this charming and suggestive quatorzain where soft sounds dominate. Night and death efface the beauty of the world and the poem ends with a hint of sadness, '. . . Je suis bien seul, / Et sombre, ô suave linceul.' (ll. 13–14). Death, which figures as a theme in 'Le Cimetière Marin', 'Fragments du Narcisse' and 'Ebauche d'un Serpent', then appears again in the beautiful ballad-like sonnet 'Le Vin Perdu', but here there is a more positive response to death than in 'La Ceinture'. Like 'La Ceinture', 'Le Vin Perdu' is concise, and charming, suggesting the secret inner life of the poet. He performs a mysterious ritual, pouring rare wine into the ocean in some forgotten place. The symbol of the wine is polyvalent, first a libation to appease the forces of death, then the poet's own blood which momentarily tints the ocean and disappears, and finally what is most precious to Valéry, his ideas. At the end of the poem this wine has transformed the ocean, made the waves drunk, and in a marvellous visionary image recalling the ending of 'Aurore', the poet sees figures leaping up into the air. Valéry's ideas, like the seeds in 'Les Grenades', have a germinating power, and if the poet and thinker dies, he still has immortality by his ideas which continue to stimulate the minds of men: 'Je m'assure que dans la voie ici indiquée, des esprits meilleurs que le mien trouveront d'assez neuves choses' (*Cahiers* I, p. 8)

III

POETICS

In 1889, Valéry wrote an article entitled 'Sur la technique littéraire' (O.I, pp. 1786–8), echoing the ideas of Edgar Allan Poe. The poet is a calculator of psychological effects in the reader, a manipulator who rejects the old Romantic image of genius seized by the delirium of inspiration:

> La littérature est l'art de se jouer de l'âme des autres. C'est avec cette brutalité scientifique que notre époque a vu poser le problème de l'esthétique du Verbe, c'est-à-dire le problème de la Forme.
>
> Etant donnés une impression, un rêve, une pensée, *il faut* l'exprimer de telle manière, qu'on produise dans l'âme d'un auditeur le maximum d'effet — et un effet entièrement calculé par l'Artiste.
>
> . . .
>
> Et, ceci nous amène naturellement à une conception toute nouvelle et moderne du poète. Ce n'est plus le délirant échevelé, celui qui écrit tout un poème dans une nuit de fièvre, c'est un froid savant, presque un algébriste, au service d'un rêveur affiné. (O.I, p. 1786)

Five years later, at the end of 'Introduction à la Méthode de Léonard de Vinci', Valéry still is referring to Poe:

> Ce qu'on appelle une *réalisation* est un véritable problème de rendement dans lequel n'entre à aucun degré le sens particulier, la clef que chaque auteur attribue à ses matériaux, mais seulement la nature de ces matériaux et l'esprit du public. Edgar Poe qui fut, dans ce siècle littéraire troublé, l'éclair même de la confusion et de l'orage poétique et de qui l'analyse s'achève parfois, comme celle de Léonard, en sourires mystérieux, a établi clairement sur la psychologie, sur la probabilité des effets, l'attaque de son lecteur. De ce point de vue, tout déplacement d'éléments fait pour être aperçu et jugé dépend de quelques lois générales et d'une appropriation particulière, définie d'avance pour une catégorie prévue d'esprits auxquels ils s'adressent spécialement; et l'œuvre d'art devient une machine destinée à exciter et à combiner les formations individuelles de ces esprits. (O.I, pp. 1197–8).

Already when this was written, however, manipulation of the reader and calculation of effects seemed to Valéry to be a sacrifice of the intellect. He had turned his main attention to a study of the functioning of the mind. When he returned to poetry in 1912 and began writing *La Jeune Parque*, it was with a mind trained by twenty years of intense activity, and as W. N. Ince has well expressed it, if inspiration as a 'free gift' was still totally rejected, inspiration as a 'conquest' was not.[1] Valéry's mature poetry depended on inspiration from a mind which had mastered its possibilities. If writing poetry still seemed at times a sacrifice of the intellect, it was also a superior 'exercise' for the mind, an activity involving the whole man, and an opportunity for self-knowledge, for observing the whole person in action:

Si au lieu d'abstraire, on maintient et on invoque, pendant le travail de l'expression, je ne sais quelle présence de l'être tout entier, de sa vie sensitive et motrice, alors la participation de ce véritable *résonateur* communique au discours de tout autres puissances, lui restitue des caractères tout primitifs. Le rythme, le geste, la collaboration de la voix par les timbres des voyelles, les accents, introduisent, en quelque sorte, le corps vivant, réagissant et agissant — et ajoutent à l'expression *finie* d'une 'pensée' ce qu'il faut pour suggérer ce qu'elle est d'autre part — la réponse, l'acte et l'instant d'un homme.[2]

If poetry is produced by the whole man, it is because Valéry's unconscious mind, his sensibility, his body participate in its creation, but above all the conscious critical part of his intellect, which transforms inspiration into *art*. Valéry's poetry is a refined art, opposed to 'life' with its superficial thoughts and facile emotions, its quotidian and transitory phenomena, its incomplete developments, incoherence and absence of form. He once wrote: 'La poésie est l'ambition d'un discours qui soit chargé de plus de sens, et mêlé de plus de musique, que le langage ordinaire n'en porte et n'en peut porter' (*Passage de Verlaine*, O.I, p. 712). Both sound and sense, the two independent aspects of language, are brought together by the poet's art into an indissoluble unity in the poem to create a mysterious 'charm' which is self-contained, unrelated to any real world. 'Vers 91, le but de la poésie me parut devoir être de produire *l'enchantement* – c'est-à-dire un état de faux équilibre et de ravissement *sans référence* AU REEL' (*Cahiers* II, p. 1125). That charm must be inexhaustible, magical, never dissipated by an understanding of what the verses are saying but always sought again and again by the reader who murmurs the lines once more to himself, profoundly feeling their meanings and their music. 'Entre autres choses interdites, je n'ai pas voulu jouer sur la surprise systématique, ni sur l'emportement éperdu, car il me paraissait que c'était réduire les effets d'un poème à l'éblouissement de l'esprit sans atteindre et satisfaire sa profondeur.'[3] The attention is neither shocked nor dispersed, but carried along by a carefully developed continuity embracing a variety of imagery, meanings and tones. Valéry uses the same or similar sounds throughout a passage or even throughout a poem. Rich rhyme, assonance and alliteration, and the unusual assonancing of masculine and feminine rhymes further create a unity of sound. Valéry rhymes more richly than any of the great French poets, and even 'enriches' rhyme by creating homophony between syllables other than the final ones: *volupté – volonté*. His ambition was 'pure poetry', something absolutely remote from what he considered to be the characteristics of prose. It was an impossible ideal but one he felt he had approached closest in a few magnificent passages such as these lines from 'Fragments du Narcisse':

> O douceur de survivre à la force du jour,
> Quand elle se retire enfin rose d'amour,
> Encore un peu brûlante, et lasse, mais comblée,
> Et de tant de trésors tendrement accablée
> Par de tels souvenirs qu'ils empourprent sa mort,
> Et qu'ils la font heureuse agenouiller dans l'or,
> Puis s'étendre, se fondre, et perdre sa vendange,
> Et s'éteindre en un songe en qui le soir se change.
>
> (II. 48–55)

Valéry distinguished himself from Mallarmé, whom he saw as exclusively preoccupied with form, and rightfully claimed that his poetry (and this would be true especially of *La Jeune Parque*) reflected his research into life and psychological functions. The above passage from *Charmes*, however, substantiates Jean Hytier's felicitous phrase that Valéry's art is above all an 'art of language'. He is essentially a 'formalist' theorist and poet who has had an important influence on criticism in France in the 1960s and 1970s. Gérard Genette, in particular, has recognized his debt to Valéry.[4] Modern critics, and Valéry, are interested in the formal, linguistic aspects of poetry, in poetry seen as a 'jeu combinatoire de langage'. This orientation excludes subjectivist expressivity, or the presence of author-as-man, as well as reference to material reality, to the 'real world'. Consideration of the author-as-man is replaced by an interest for language manifesting itself through the agency of the writer,[5] while reference to the real world is effaced by a belief in the book as 'écriture'.

Valéry's poetic language, however, is a personal one, limited, created by conscious choice, immediately recognizable. (Valéry once explained why he had stopped writing and publishing poetry by saying that he had worn out his poetic vocabulary.) Yet at the same time this language is also impersonal, because it is the poem itself which seems to speak, rather than the poet, even in lines such as 'Dormeuse, amas doré d'ombres et d'abandons' addressed to a sleeping mistress in 'La Dormeuse'. 'Lorsqu' une œuvre est très belle elle perd son auteur. Elle n'est plus sa propriété. Elle convient à tous. Elle dévore son père – Il n'en fut que le moyen. Elle le dépouille' (*Cahiers* II, p. 990). Many terms are excluded from this language:

A mon sentiment, il est essentiel d'exclure de la poésie (*en général*), tous les mots avec lesquels on ne pense pas. Les *mots* qui *seraient ridicules à chanter*. Les mots non familiers à la pensée, comme irradier etc. Les mots qui ne viennent pas sans sembler être cherchés. Il faut du travail pour leur faire la chasse et simuler les premiers termes de la *pensée à l'état naissant*. Simulation aussi savante que l'on peut, de la pensée à l'état naissant. C'est poésie.[6]

Another note explains how Valéry makes his choices:

La plus belle poésie a la voix d'une femme idéale, Mlle Ame. Pour môi la voix intérieure me sert de repère. Je rejette tout ce qu'elle refuse, comme *exagéré*; car la voix intérieure ne supporte que les paroles dont le sens est secrètement d'accord avec l'être *vrai*: dont la musique est le graphique même des mouvements et arrêts de cet être.

(*Cahiers* II, p.1076)

There is only a limited use of rare words, mostly from classical antiquity, some archaic terms, no neologisms. On the other hand, popular and familiar expressions are virtually excluded, although we do find the colloquial 'ni vu, ni connu' in 'Le Sylphe', but transformed by Valéry's poetic genius and brilliant variations from stanza to stanza. Valéry's vocabulary tends toward general and noble terms, a rather surprising fact in the first quarter of the twentieth century. As Pierre Guiraud comments: 'Cette double tendance est remarquable à une époque qui recherche au contraire le terme particulier et qui, depuis le Romantisme, s'est efforcé de proscrire un langage jugé conventionnel.'[7]

Valéry's poetic vocabulary may be limited, but because of his Symbolist origins, the range of meanings is very large. Valéry himself commented on the varied suggestions arising from such words as *liberté* or *spirituel*, as contrasted with a limited word such as *pain*.[8] He renews words or expressions as in 'au point doré de périr' in 'La Ceinture', and the 'étrange oisiveté, mais pleine de pouvoir' of 'Le Cimetière Marin'. Still another expansion of meaning, as Albert Henry has shown in his lexicon,[9] results from the simultaneous use of the current and etymological meaning of a word. Valéry, like Mallarmé and Baudelaire before him, was also sensitive to the magical effect of several evocative words coming together in a verse, such as 'Orient', 'désert', and 'ennui'. Even the metrical pattern can affect the sense of a word by emphasizing it and causing it to hover over an entire line. Valéry often practised the 1/5 division of an alexandrine hemistich, frequently augmenting the accentuation further by the use of sounds as in 'Sa voix fraîche à mes vœux *tremble* de consentir', or 'Des cimes, l'air déjà *cesse* le pur pillage' (my italics), two of many examples of this technique in 'Fragments du Narcisse'.

Such a calculated technique suggests something about Valéry's way of writing poetry. Constantly he emphasized the importance of judgement, awareness, and self-criticism, of effort and the creation of obstacles – the use of arbitrary conventions of prosody, classical forms and metres, as well as his own exigencies – to increase the amount of thought and work between inspiration and finished verses.[10] One of the themes of Valéry's poetics is the separation he makes between the poet as producer of inspirations on one hand and the poet as chooser and architect on the other. Inspiration, however, is still essential. The mature Valéry no longer sees the poet as simply a manipulator of the reader. It is W. N. Ince who probably best describes how various kinds of inspiration occurred to Valéry and what he did with them.[11] The first stage was an 'état poétique' which Valéry has analysed in a well-known passage:

L'état ou émotion poétique me semble consister dans une perception naissante, dans une tendance à percevoir un *monde*, ou système complet de rapports, dans lequel les êtres, les choses, les événements et les actes, s'ils ressemblent, *chacun à chacun*, à ceux qui peuplent et composent le monde sensible, le monde immédiat duquel ils sont empruntés, sont, d'autre part, dans une relation indéfinissable, mais merveilleusement juste, avec les modes et les lois de notre sensibilité générale. Alors, ces objets et ces êtres connus changent en quelque sorte de valeur. Ils s'appellent les uns les autres, ils s'associent tout autrement que dans les conditions ordinaires. Ils se trouvent, — permettez-moi cette expression, — *musicalisés*, devenus commensurables, résonants l'un par l'autre. ('Propos sur la Poésie', O.I, p. 1363)

The terms Valéry uses to describe his poetic state are important, not the least by the limited role given to the imagination. If Valéry refused the shock and surprise effects and discontinuity of imagery of the Surrealists, he also refused their extraordinary imagination as well as the visions of Rimbaud:

Tandis que tels poètes (Rimb[aud] etc.) ont plutôt visé à donner l'impression d'un *état* extraordinaire (*vision* — résonance réciproque des choses — exploration désespérée des sens, et de l'expression) d'autres, et moi, avons cherché à donner l'idée d'un '*monde*' ou système des choses bien plus séparé du monde commun — mais fait de ses éléments les mêmes — les liaisons seules étant choisies — et aussi les définitions — Ceci par éliminations beaucoup plus serrées. Mais en refusant à ce point, on refuse du très puissant. (*Cahiers* II, p. 1116)

It is from the poetic state that an inspiration may arise, a group of words as in 'Pâle, profondément mordue' which resulted in 'La Pythie', or a rhythm empty of content, as was the case with 'Le Cimetière Marin', where a decasyllabic rhythm was eventually fleshed out with the words of a verse.[12] Valéry emphasizes, however, that such inspirations are not necessarily acceptable to the critical eye of the poet. In rare cases they may be already in perfect shape, but often they are totally useless, or else in need of much work. Still, the best of these initial inspirations serve as ideal models when the poet is later obliged to create other verses by dint of hard work.

As Ince has shown, a successful initial inspiration is followed by a period of 'intimation', or the conviction that with some effort and patience a certain poetic vein is there to be exploited. This is a stage requiring the exertion of will and the expenditure of effort, but not too much effort, and then waiting and even forgetting while unconscious processes function. Never, however, does the subconscious 'take over' and dominate the situation. Christine Crow has further pursued Ince's analysis to show that there is a collaboration in Valéry's mind between the conscious and the unconscious, a maintenance of that unity of the intellect so important to Valéry.[13] The unconscious does exist for Valéry, and it does furnish words of the poem, and may seem to operate independently, as, for instance, in 'Palme'. But as Christine Crow has shown, all the functioning of the unconscious in the state of intimation has been 'conditioned' by the operations of the conscious mind, and, of course, anything emerging from the unconscious is immediately subject to scrutiny, evaluation, and alteration by the alert intellect.

Eventually 'intimation' wore off, exhausted itself, and Valéry was obliged to resort to 'vers calculés', verses made by 'headwork' and derived from an exploitation of language, from clusters of words he would jot down on his manuscript. Such verses, consciously 'fabricated', were then 'naturalized' by the poet to become consonant with the lines obtained by inspiration and intimation. After a period of 'fabrication', with a movement in a certain direction, the state of intimation might again return, and even new inspirations. Furthermore at any time during the creative process, complete surprises could occur, producing all kinds of new possibilities. They occurred so inevitably, that Valéry *counted* on their appearance.

It is no doubt obvious by now that Valéry did not usually complete his poems in one sitting but by discontinuous operations devoted to a slow reshaping of the products of his sensibility, to the arduous creation of 'vers calculés', and of course to composition. Composition to Valéry meant a high degree of integration of parts. It began with the union of sound and sense and in the relationship of successive sounds, the creation of that unity of sound we have already described. It would be wrong, therefore, to think only of composition in its simple prosaic sense, a structure of ideas. It would also be erroneous to imagine any simple form of composition governing the unfolding of a Valerian poem. Perhaps the analogy of symphonic composition, favoured by Valéry and Claudel, communicates what Valéry was trying to achieve. The structure of the poem became a complex system of movements, with allusions from one part to another, symmetries, contrasts, and similarities. Valéry excluded chronological and 'logical' composition, as well as composition by association. The unfolding of the poem had to appear at the same time continuous and yet unexpected. As I have pointed out in the 'Athlone French Poets' edition of *Charmes* (p. 90), Valéry re-arranged, for instance, the stanzas of 'Aurore', apparently to obtain an unexpected movement from the second to the third stanza, far more interesting than the prior arrangement where the garden imagery of stanza two was prolonged in what is now stanza seven.

Although Valéry sometimes had some kind of general plan in the early stages of creation, as seems to have been the case with 'Le Cimetière Marin', generally his attitude toward the proliferation of his poem was highly flexible. *La Jeune Parque* started as a forty-line poem, as we have noted, and grew to 512 lines. Valéry was capable of changing direction as the poem advanced, inspired by some consideration, formal or cognitive, to a new departure. The need to join two separate fragments could produce a new passage and a new development. Passages changed position in *La Jeune Parque* and 'Le Cimetière Marin', and in the case of 'La Pythie' and 'Ebauche d'un Serpent', verses moved from one poem to another. Valéry found it extremely important to maintain a state of disorder as long as possible, not imprisoning himself in one line of development. Finally, however, he does perfect and finish the poem, carefully effacing in the final stage everything revealing or suggesting the acts of fabrication. At the same time, Valéry affirms that a poem is never really 'finished' because the poet can always take it up again and make changes. 'Féerie' and 'Même Féerie' in the *Album de Vers Anciens* reveal a Valéry tempted by variations. He changed the ending of 'Ebauche d'un Serpent' after its initial publication, and he would have liked to work on this great poem even longer. He changed the order of the first ten stanzas of 'Le Cimetière Marin' between first publication in the *N.R.F.* and its publication in a pamphlet three months later.

The reader, however, according to Valéry, should have the feeling in reading a poem that nothing could be modified, that no improvement is possible. Valéry himself had this feeling one day when he found himself reading some lines of poetry in an

opened book in a shop window. They resisted his every attempt
to alter them. The lines were from *Phèdre* by Racine. Beyond this
impression of perfection, Valéry limits the certain effects he hopes
to obtain through the poem. Again he has evolved from the Poe-
inspired theories of his youth which had envisaged a high degree
of control over the reader. He still thinks constantly of the reader
as he composes the poem, and an artwork which has called upon
the totality of the poet in order to be created will be destined to
appeal to the total being of the reader, even, through rhythms,
to his body. This control, however, remains general, and
Valéry claims there is no direct communication from poet to
reader. Direct communication, in fact, would diminish the
poem, reducing its possible effects. Valéry counts on the reader's
contribution to the meaning of his poem and at times even claims
to see value in 'errors' and 'misunderstandings' created by his
readers. Again Valéry reveals himself as a Symbolist poet,
refusing to fix and limit the sense of his poems.

It would no doubt be too much to expect that he could accept
all interpretations. Certainly the third stanza of 'Le Sylphe'
gently mocks those who failed to understand his poems, although
here he is no doubt mostly aiming at those who rejected them
altogether. In the private notes of his *Cahiers*, Valéry attacked
those who thought 'Les Pas' an allegory of approaching inspiration, and revealed his own intention: 'petit poème purement
sentimental' (*Cahiers* II, p. 1054). Julien P. Monod, who acted for
many years as secretary to Valéry, once said to me that Valéry
had told him that Alain had not understood his poetry. But perhaps not too much importance should be attributed to Valéry
possibly contradicting his own theories. His fundamental position
is certainly revealed in this passage from the *Cahiers*:

L'affaire du poète est de construire une sorte de corps verbal qui ait la
solidité, mais l'ambiguïté, d'un objet. L'expérience montre qu'un
poème trop simple (p. ex. abstrait) est *insuffisant* et s'use à la première
vue. Ce n'est plus même un poème. Le pouvoir d'être repris et resucé
dépend du nombre d'interprétations compatibles avec le texte et ce
nombre résulte lui-même d'une netteté qui impose l'obligation d'inter-
préter et d'une indétermination qui la repousse. (*Cahiers* II, p. 1074).

SEVEN PROSE WORKS

LA SOIREE AVEC MONSIEUR TESTE

Paul Valéry wrote one of his most famous and fascinating works, 'La Soirée avec Monsieur Teste', when he was not quite twenty-three years old, in the month of August 1894, at Montpellier, in the apartment where Auguste Comte spent his childhood, and it remains today as the most celebrated work in all the 'Teste cycle', notes and short pieces which Valéry composed during the rest of his life.[1] 'La Soirée' is in part inspired by literary sources, Balzac's *Louis Lambert*,[2] as well as 'The Murders in the Rue Morgue' and other stories of Edgar Allan Poe detailing the brilliant deductions of the master logician Auguste Dupin. On the other hand, Teste was also modelled on Valéry's idea of the severe and rigorous intellectual existence of the painter Degas. Monsieur Teste certainly represents an extreme intellectual ideal toward which Valéry was striving, an absolute, a 'mystique' for this mind which rejected all mystiques.[3] In an important preface in 1925, Valéry recalls the extraordinary state in which he composed 'La Soirée':

Teste fut engendré, . . . pendant une ère d'ivresse de ma volonté et parmi d'étranges excès de conscience de soi.

J'étais affecté du mal aigu de la précision. Je tendais à l'extrême du désir insensé de comprendre, et je cherchais en moi les points critiques de ma faculté d'attention.

Je faisais donc ce que je pouvais pour augmenter un peu les durées de quelques pensées. Tout ce qui m'était facile m'était indifférent et presque ennemi. La sensation de l'effort me semblait devoir être recherchée, et je ne prisais pas les heureux résultats qui ne sont que les fruits naturels de nos vertus natives. C'est dire que les résultats en général, — et par conséquence, les *œuvres*, — m'importaient beaucoup moins que l'énergie de l'ouvrier . . . (O.II, p. 11)

To understand 'La Soirée', it is useful perhaps to imagine a triangle with a series of hurdles up one side. The young Valéry is situated somewhere close to the bottom of these hurdles, while Teste is near the peak. The figure represents first of all an upward-thrusting, increasing intellectual power which reaches its maximum possibilities at the summit. At the same time, the progressive narrowing of the triangle suggests a continuing liberation of the self from all imaginable encumbrances hindering the free operation of the intellect, such as material possessions, prejudices, conventions, vanity, ambitions, inhibitions, fears, melancholy, and other aspects of the personality. Even the problems the mind solves are left behind, once they are understood. 'Et que m'importe ce que je sais fort bien?', asks Monsieur Teste (O.II, p. 19). Constant rejection and liberation with a constant increase of intellectual power. 'Que peut un homme?' is the key question several times repeated throughout the text (O.II, p. 23). Teste is the symbol of intellectual *possibility*:

> J'ai posé cette question, il y a plus de 50 ans — *Que peut un homme?* (Teste) . . . Quant à moi, *jusqu'au bout* fut mon désir 1° en fait d'*intellect* — arriver par manœuvres et exercices d'imagination et self-conscience à former l'idée de nos possibilités . . . (*Cahiers* I, p. 231)

The functioning of this programme depends on a positive attitude toward the intellect which sees it as a closed system without any magical interventions such as 'inspiration', 'divinity', and 'genius'. Teste refuses such mysteries and abdications. Once the reality of the brain and its operations has been recognized, an increase in intellectual power depends mightily on self-awareness, self-study, and it is a theme repeatedly voiced by 'La Soirée' from the opening lines where the laconic and disabused narrator proclaims: 'Je me suis rarement perdu de vue' (O.II, p. 15), to the very last lines where Teste falling asleep anticipates a famous line of *La Jeune Parque*: 'Je suis étant, et me voyant; me voyant me voir. . .' (O.II, p. 25).[4] Self-awareness discovers those laws of the mind which will increase its powers and most efficiently mature ideas, and then the mind must learn those laws, adopt them, make them habitual. There is a strong theme of self-training, self-transformation in 'La Soirée'. 'Trouver n'est rien. Le difficile est de s'ajouter ce qu'on trouve' (O.II, p. 17). It is all a very 'inhuman' programme, and Valéry seems well aware of how rigorous it is. 'J'entrevoyais des sentiments qui me faisaient frémir, une terrible obstination dans des expériences enivrantes' (O.II, p. 18).

Teste's memory is no indiscriminate warehouse. It automatically rids itself of useless encumbrances, retaining only the indispensable. 'Certainement sa mémoire singulière devait presque uniquement lui retenir cette partie de nos impressions que notre imagination toute seule est impuissante à construire' (O.II, p. 18).[5] He thinks in his own language, rejecting conventional speech, the language of others, unsuited to unique thought. And thought begins with genuine *observation*, freed from clichés, ready-made concepts.[6] The text itself exemplifies original observation and expression when Teste and the narrator go to the Opera: 'Une immense fille de cuivre nous séparait d'un groupe murmurant au delà de l'éblouissement. Au fond de la vapeur, brillait un morceau nu de femme, doux comme un caillou. Beaucoup d'éventails indépendants vivaient sur le monde sombre et clair, écumant jusqu'aux feux du haut' (O.II, p. 20). Teste and the narrator are fascinated by the classification of the audience, by the laws governing the behaviour of this vast auditorium.[7] But Teste resists the fascination of the spectacle (apparently Wagner's *Die Walkyrie*)[8] and the paralysing effects of anything extraordinary: 'Je suis chez MOI, je parle ma langue, je hais les choses extraordinaires. C'est le besoin des esprits faibles' (O. II, p. 22).

But is Teste entirely inhuman? Neither he nor the narrator are shown as invulnerable. Early in the story, the narrator, in many ways already a 'little Teste', says that he is growing old, that he has even had several close brushes with death. Then he tells us that he once met Teste in 'une sorte de b. . .' (O.II, p. 17), and Valéry explains in his *Cahiers* that he added this allusion to a bordello to compensate, by a single letter, 'la couleur abstraite du texte, et donner aussi économiquement que possible un accent de liberté de mœurs assez vulgaire — ou de libertinage à mon "héros" de l'intellect'.[9] When Teste emerges from the Opera, he complains slightly of the coolness of the air and mentions 'd'anciennes douleurs' (O.II, p. 22). A few minutes later, in his sparsely furnished room, he too says: 'Je suis vieux', and then he is seized with intense pain, and the entire ending of 'La Soirée' is largely occupied with this suffering, and then with sleep, and even suggestions of death. Valéry did not make his Teste some entirely unreal being beyond the demands of the body. There may be contempt expressed for biological life,[10] for the 'events' of life, for life in society, but there is also a certain facing up to life's demands and limits. Possibly Valéry drew on his own early attacks of severe neuralgia,[11] but he relied no doubt as much on his constant awareness of all that limits the intelligence. Through this awareness he triumphed, at least to a degree, over those limits. Already the narrator, in his brushes with death, tried to scrutinize the situation, 'anxieux d'épuiser, d'éclairer quelque situation douloureuse' (O.II, p. 15). Later, when he talks of the possibility of Teste in love, or ill, or afraid, he adds: 'Il aime, il souffre, il s'ennuie. Tout le monde s'imite. Mais, au soupir, au gémissement élémentaire, je veux qu'il mêle les règles et les figures de tout son esprit' (O.II, p. 20). This is just what happens in the last scene of 'La Soirée'. Without losing any of its poignant reality for the reader, physical pain is intellectualized by Teste: 'Voyez-vous ces figures vives? cette géométrie de ma souffrance' (O.II, p. 24). His mind had already foreseen his illness: 'Sachez que j'avais prévu la maladie future' (O.II, p. 25). Even in these moments of torment which will finally defeat him, Teste can utter again his famous question: 'Que peut un homme?' (O.II, p. 25).

INTRODUCTION A LA METHODE DE LEONARD DE VINCI

Valéry began the 'Introduction à la Méthode de Léonard de Vinci' late in 1894, the year of 'La Soirée avec Monsieur Teste', and like 'La Soirée', it develops the idea of an ideal intellect. At the beginning of this important essay, first published in *La Nouvelle Revue* in 1895, Valéry makes it clear that the 'Introduction' has little to do with the historical Leonardo, although there is an emphasis in the essay on architectural construction, suggesting that Leonardo might be a contrast to Teste, who created no works. This contrast, however, should not be unduly emphasized because both texts are essentially concerned with the same thing: not with creations, but with the operations of a powerful universal intellect, exercising all its faculties and *capable* of creation, both artistic and scientific. Unlike Bergson, Valéry believed there was no conflict between the practice of positive science and complete action of the mind, and like Descartes, he emphasized the importance of a trained mind rather than merely an erudite one.

This mind begins with observation, continues with the analytical and imaginative manipulation of mental imagery, and ends with construction. To observe reality, the observer must rid himself of preconceived ideas, of clichés which substitute a stock of concepts for genuine vision. Unfortunately, for most people, 'une forme cubique, blanchâtre, en hauteur, et trouée de reflets de vitres est immédiatement une maison, pour eux: la Maison!' (O.I, p. 1165). True observation must be personal, subjective, alert to various perspectives. There is a reflection here of late nineteenth-century scientific thinking when there was much concern with the problems of knowing reality, and much importance given to the role of the subjective observer. A long development near the beginning of the essay gives a detailed account of the changing vision of the observer as he fixes his gaze on the reality before him. 'Et voici lentement [certaines formes] qui commencent de se faire oublier, et de ne plus être vues qu'à peine, tandis que d'autres parviennent à se faire apercevoir, – là où elles avaient toujours été' (O.I, p. 1168). Such intense attention to perception produces fragments of fresh and original vision, and Valéry mocks those who fail to observe. 'Si le bout d'un nez, un éclat d'épaule, deux doigts trempent au hasard dans un coup de lumière qui les isole, eux ne se font jamais à n'y voir qu'un bijou neuf, enrichissant leur vision' (O.I, p. 1166). The passage recalls, of course, the brilliant imagery of the Opera section in 'La Soirée avec Monsieur Teste': 'Au fond de la vapeur, brillait un morceau nu de femme, doux comme un caillou' (O.II, p. 20).

The observer tries to preserve the freshness of sense data, while in a second stage the intellect exercises its powers of analysis and imagination. This analyst, however, must be a universal mind circulating freely across the boundaries of intellectual disciplines, being both artist and scientist like Leonardo da Vinci.[12] In a page of powerful contempt for the limited vision of the modern-day specialist, Valéry presents his greatest argument for universality:

Neuf fois sur dix, toute grande nouveauté dans un ordre est obtenue par l'intrusion de moyens et de notions qui n'y étaient pas prévus; venant d'attribuer ces progrès à la formation d'images, puis de langages, nous ne pouvons éluder cette conséquence que la quantité de ces langages possédée par un homme, influe singulièrement sur le nombre des chances qu'il peut avoir d'en trouver de nouveaux. (O.I, p. 1180)

It is the human mind with its own powers which achieves this universality; once again Valéry takes a positive view of the intellect and refuses mysterious and marvellous words such as 'genius' and 'inspiration'. Nor does the great thinker seem to derive from a nation, a group, or a tradition. He is isolated, independent, unlimited, original. In like manner Valéry turns away from the dead weight of the past, history and erudition. Instead of a cluttered and encumbered mind, he envisages an intellect straining toward the future, dynamic, and fully equipped for thought.[13] He even dreams of a method for foreseeing at the start all the results of a thought or action, thus permitting the mind to move quickly from early stages of a reflection to final ones:

L'idée surgit alors, (ou le désir), de précipiter le cours de cette suite, d'en porter les termes à leur *limite*, à celle de leurs expressions imaginables, *après laquelle tout sera changé*. Et si ce mode d'être conscient devient habituel, on en viendra, par exemple, à examiner d'emblée tous les résultats possibles d'un acte envisagé, tous les rapports d'un objet conçu, pour arriver de suite à s'en défaire, à la faculté de deviner toujours une chose plus intense ou plus exacte que la chose donnée, au pouvoir de se réveiller hors d'une pensée qui durait trop. (O.I, p. 1162)

In a note, Valéry credits the great mathematician Henri Poincaré (1854–1912) with this idea, and the 'Introduction' throughout is very much influenced by Poincaré's thought, as both Sutcliffe and Laurette have demonstrated.[14]

Toward the end of the essay, again no doubt influenced by Poincaré, who was aware of the importance of intuitions even in logic, Valéry describes the 'imaginative logic' of Faraday, an inductive process utilizing mental images. Such use of the imagination is the greatest triumph of the creative intellect, and is the essential aspect of Leonardo's method. Its importance for Valéry is confirmed by a note on Faraday in a *Cahier* for 1942, nearly a half-century after the composition of the 'Introduction':

Images
Dear Faraday!
Le triomphe de l'image mentale — Transposition de l'image physique dans le champ mental.

Et ICI, cette image qui visuellement est une figure inerte, prend des 'forces'. *L'œil ne voit pas de forces* — c'est l'excitation de nos puissances motrices qui entre en jeu — dans le champ-de-temps mental.

L'image est mieux qu'une réplique, les yeux fermés, d'un objet visible. Elle prend valeur d'excitant d'un développement et devient par là un élément de quelque construction qui la dépasse, — dont elle est un effet, un cas particulier, un indice.

Elle s'est développée ainsi dans un *implexe* — comme un germe cristallin. Mais il y faut une solution — et sursaturée. Ou comme une graine.

(II, pp. 909–10)

Successful utilization of this or other methods, however, depends on the degree of critical awareness of mental imagery existing in the mind, and this self-awareness is the key to the 'Introduction' as it is, of course, to all of Valéry's thought:

La conscience des pensées que l'on a, en tant que ce sont des pensées, est de reconnaître cette sorte d'égalité ou d'homogénéité; de sentir que toutes les combinaisons de la sorte sont légitimes, naturelles, et que la méthode consiste à les exciter, à les voir avec précision, à chercher ce qu'elles impliquent. (O.I, p. 1162)

The study of mental processes in the 'Introduction' culminates, as will 'Eupalinos' in 1921, with architectural construction, where the creative mind must be both artist and scientist. In the discussion of the joys and problems of construction, Valéry placed a significant passage on the 'ornamental', or formalist, conception of art. This view considers the elements entering the art work not by their significance but by the way they relate to each other. Once again Valéry parallels Poincaré and the importance he gave not to the study of objects, but to relationships between them. It is the creative intellect which discovers these relationships, and this returns us to Valéry's major preoccupation in 1894 and the years following, and also to the theme which dominates this essay: the complex functioning of the human mind.

NOTE ET DIGRESSION

In 1919, Valéry wrote a sequel, entitled 'Note et Digression', to his 'Introduction à la Méthode de Léonard de Vinci' of 1894. The passage of twenty-five years, and the evolution of the young man of twenty-three to the middle-aged man of forty-eight have

brought their changes. Whereas Valéry did not discuss himself
as a poet in the earlier text (he had just turned his major attention away from literature), in 1919 he examines the self-critical,
self-conscious writer at some length. He had published *La Jeune
Parque* in 1917, and the poems of *Charmes* were already appearing in
various periodicals. If he displays considerable assurance and
even lapidary phrases in this passage 'L'enthousiasme n'est pas
un état d'âme d'écrivain' (O.I, p. 1205), the beginning of 'Note
et Digression' has a modesty which did not characterize the
younger Valéry's 'Introduction'. In the opening paragraph, he
calls his earlier title 'ambitieux' and 'trompeur'. As for the text,
'on ne songerait même pas à l'écrire' (O.I, p. 1199). Later, half-
way through this new essay, he makes an unequivocal statement
about the limits of the human intellect:

Même notre pensée la plus 'profonde' est contenue dans les conditions
invincibles qui font que toute pensée est 'superficielle'. On ne pénètre
que dans une forêt de transpositions; ou bien c'est un palais fermé de
miroirs, que féconde une lampe solitaire qu'ils enfantent à l'infini.

(O. I, pp. 1215–16)

Limits of thought was not a theme of the earlier essay, but it was
something to which Valéry had given considerable attention
between 1894 and 1919. The paradoxical image of the closed
palace with infinite reflections parallels exactly the famous image
of the cistern and boundless space representing the human mind
and body, inclosed and yet unfathomable, in the eighth stanza
of 'Le Cimetière Marin': 'Amère, sombre et sonore citerne/
Sonnant dans l'âme un creux toujours futur!' (ll. 47–8). Death
is another new theme in 'Note et Digression', although there were
suggestions of it in the last pages of 'La Soirée avec Monsieur
Teste'. Here death is not merely suggested, but dwelled upon
through several pages:

Cette pente fait pressentir qu'elle peut devenir irrésistible; elle prononce
le commencement d'un éloignement sans retour du soleil spirituel, du
maximum admirable de la netteté, de la solidité, du pouvoir de distinguer
et de choisir; on la devine qui s'abaisse, obscurcie de mille impuretés
psychologiques, obsédée de bourdons et de vertiges, à travers la confusion
des temps et le trouble des fonctions, et qui se dirige défaillante au
milieu d'un désordre inexprimable des *dimensions* de la connaissance,

jusqu'à l'état instantané et indivis qui étouffe ce chaos dans la nullité.

(O.I, pp. 1218-19)

Death is also a powerful theme in *La Jeune Parque*, first appearing in ll. 141-8 and then, with the sexual theme, dominant throughout the rest of the poem. Death is again a major theme in 'Le Cimetière Marin', ll. 52-120. Still, *La Jeune Parque*, 'Le Cimetière Marin', and 'Note et Digression' all end with a powerful affirmation, although the ending of 'Note et Digression' is so extreme that it recalls more the exalted intellectual dominance of the beginning of 'Le Cimetière Marin' where the protagonist stands face to face with the noonday sun:

> L'âme exposée aux torches du solstice,
> Je te soutiens, admirable justice
> De la lumière aux armes sans pitié!
> Je te rends pure à ta place première:
> Regarde-toi! . . .
>
> (ll. 37-41)

In 'Note et Digression', Valéry writes:

[La conscience] se pose enfin comme fille directe et ressemblante de l'être sans visage, sans origine, auquel incombe et se rapporte toute la tentative du cosmos . . . Encore un peu, et elle ne compterait plus comme existences nécessaires que deux entités essentiellement inconnues: Soi et X. Toutes deux abstraites de tout, impliquées dans tout, impliquant tout. Egales et consubstantielles. (O.I, pp. 1222-3)

The entire last half of 'Note et Digression' develops the idea of the *Moi Pur*, a pure and unencumbered capacity for thinking, and opposes it to death, to the real world, and even to ideas generated by the mind and all its past accomplishments. The *Moi Pur* is oriented toward future possibility rather than past actions. It is characterized by a perpetual exhaustion and rejection of problems, by a 'refus d'être quoi que ce soit' (O.I, p. 1225). It is radically distinguished from the personality, that lesser deity subject to vanity and created by accidents. Such detachment permitted the originality of a Leonardo in his ideas on love and death. Valéry approves his contempt for the grotesqueness of the sexual act, and approves also the idea that death is a tragedy for the *soul*, deprived of the marvellous human body. 'Rien de plus libre, c'est-à-dire, rien de moins humain, que ses jugements sur l'amour, sur la mort' (O.I, p. 1212). But Valéry is not primarily interested in giving us Leonardo's ideas in this essay. Like the 'Introduction' which preceded it, 'Note et Digression' is oriented toward an exploration of the functioning of the mind itself. The 1919 essay, however, with its juxtaposition of human limits and extreme affirmation, is far more dramatic than the 'Introduction', and closer in theme and structure to the two great poems of 1917 and 1920.

EUPALINOS OU L'ARCHITECTE

'Eupalinos' was completed by Valéry on 4 March 1921, more than seven months before the abrupt end of his love affair with Catherine Pozzi, and there is a possible echo of the happy side of this liaison in comments Eupalinos makes on his little temple to Hermes:

> Où le passant ne voit qu'une élégante chapelle, — c'est peu de chose: quatre colonnes, un style très simple, — j'ai mis le souvenir d'un clair jour de ma vie. O douce métamorphose! Ce temple délicat, nul ne le sait, est l'image mathématique d'une fille de Corinthe, que j'ai heureusement aimée. Il en reproduit fidèlement les proportions particulières. Il vit pour moi! Il me rend ce que je lui ai donné. . . (O.II, p. 92)

More important, however, than this link with Valéry's personal life is the connection between 'Eupalinos' and 'Le Cimetière Marin'. It is almost impossible not to think of the first stanzas of this poem in the opening pages of the dialogue where Valéry explores the perspective of the changing world of men seen from the point of view of Eternity. The opposition of immobility to change is the essential theme of 'Le Cimetière Marin'. In the dialogue, however, the point of view is completely reversed, and the Absolute, instead of being something supremely valuable, is shown to be quite inadequate. Socrates in Eternity can no longer understand life. 'Je plaçais la Sagesse dans la posture éternelle où nous sommes. Mais d'ici tout est méconnaissable. La vérité est devant nous, et nous ne comprenons plus rien' (O.II, p. 81). 'Eupalinos' is a dialogue not about the perfection of the Absolute, but about the joys and wonders of a transitory existence. Phaedrus rejects Plato's idea of an ideal beauty and proclaims instead that 'rien de beau n'est séparable de la vie, et la vie est ce qui meurt'

(O.II, p. 88). Socrates is continually aware of everything he has lost, particularly the body with all its marvellous capacities, praised here even more than in 'Note et Digression'. In the seventh and eighth stanzas of 'Le Cimetière Marin' that same body is only a 'morne moitié' (l. 42), an 'amère, sombre et sonore citerne' (l. 47) whose impenetrable mysteries prevent a complete self-knowledge, self-mastery, intellectual purity.

'Eupalinos' is closer to the concluding stanzas and the epigraph of 'Le Cimetière Marin' taken from Pindar, 'No dear soul, do not aspire to some eternal life, but exhaust what you can accomplish in reality.' The real accomplishments which form a major theme of the dialogue are construction, architecture, 'formal' art. Several key passages communicate the importance of form, not only in architecture, but also in Valéry's poetry, for in many ways Eupalinos the architect, hero of the dialogue, is an artist who closely resembles Valéry the poet. The very first precept of Eupalinos which Phaedrus repeats to Socrates is '*Il n'y a point de détails dans l'exécution*' (O.II, p. 84), which is simply another way of saying that form is what is important, whether it be the way two parts of a building are harmoniously juxtaposed in a skilful modulation, or whether it be the placing of silences and the grouping of sounds in a poem or discourse. The reference to architectural modulations (O.II, p. 86) recalls what was perhaps the greatest formal problem in the execution of *La Jeune Parque*:

une recherche, littéralement indéfinie, de ce qu'on pourrait tenter en poésie qui fût analogue à ce qu'on nomme 'modulation', en musique . . . Rien, d'ailleurs ne m'intéresse plus dans les arts que ces transitions où je vois ce qu'il y a de plus délicat et de plus savant à accomplir . . .

(O.I, p. 1473).

On the artist's skill depends the enchantment of the viewer or reader. '*Il faut que mon temple meuve les hommes comme les meut l'objet aimé*', said Eupalinos (O.II, p. 87), causing Phaedrus and Socrates to discuss the nature of that 'charm' which for Valéry was the effect of the work of art. It emerges from the purity of the means employed, sweeping the viewer away from his human condition and elevating him 'sans effort, au-dessus de sa nature' (O.II, p. 89), and it remains finally mysterious, magical, indefinable, inexhaustible, like the magical and fleeting image of the woman's breast in the final stanza of 'Le Sylphe':

Ni vu ni connu,
Le temps d'un sein nu
Entre deux chemises!

Through Socrates, Valéry emphasizes that this 'charm' should never astonish or shock the reader. Instead it must be 'ce qui doit l'émerveiller sans le confondre, le posséder sans l'abêtir' (O.II, p. 89). While the Surrealists sought deliberately effects of shock in order to jar the reader out of his routine habits and thus expand his mind, Valéry avoided these same effects so that the reader's mind would function to the maximum of its capabilities.

Socrates regrets never having cultivated the architect he felt within himself, and Valéry with his typical scepticism for moral teachings, amuses himself by making him disavow his entire life: 'Qu'ai-je donc fait que de donner à croire au reste des humains que j'en savais bien plus qu'eux-mêmes sur les choses les plus douteuses?' (O.II, p. 139). At the same time, Valéry embarks on another of his favourite themes, possibility, a theme which appeared in Monsieur Teste's repeated phrase 'Que peut un homme?' (O.II, p. 23). Socrates, however, takes a more pessimistic perspective:

Je t'ai dit que je suis né *plusieurs*, et que je suis mort, *un seul*. L'enfant qui vient est une foule innombrable, que la vie réduit assez tôt à un seul individu, celui qui se manifeste et qui meurt. Une quantité de Socrates est née avec moi, d'où, peu à peu, se détacha le Socrate qui était dû aux magistrats et à la ciguë. (O.II, p. 114)

No doubt Valéry himself also felt some regret for the architect he might have been. We think of his 'Paradoxe sur l'Architecte' (O.II, pp. 1402–5), which dates from 1891, his lyrical praise of architectural construction in 'Introduction à la Méthode de Léonard de Vinci' (O.I, pp. 1188–92), 'Orphée' (O.I, pp. 76–7), 'Amphion' (O.I, pp. 166–81), 'Air de Sémiramis' (O.I, pp. 91–4), and of course his poem in *Charmes*, 'Le Cantique des Colonnes'. If Valéry sacrificed a possibility, however, the sacrifice was not complete, because as we have already remarked, Eupalinos resembles Valéry very much. The similarity occurs not only in their art, but also in their attitude toward the intellect. Like Valéry, Eupalinos is interested in *how* things are produced, in the process of generation by the human mind. Eupalinos is as aware of the various processes of the creating mind as Valéry himself. And when Eupalinos says: 'A force de construire, je crois bien que je me suis construit moi-même' (O.II, p. 92), he recalls an important remark Valéry made about *La Jeune Parque*: 'Lorsque j'ai terminé ma *Jeune Parque*, en avril 1917, ce poème m'a laissé dans un état d'entraînement intellectuel et littéraire acquis par quatre ans d'un travail assidu' (O.I, p. 1614).

Toward the end of the dialogue, Valéry introduces another architect, Tridon le Sidonien, builder of ships, whose presence here is justified first of all by the memory of Ancient Greece which constructed not only temples but also navies and merchant vessels. Tridon is being used as a dramatic and picturesque extension of Eupalinos in order to close the dialogue with particularly forceful emphasis on qualities of mind which were important for Valéry. He is more an artisan than Eupalinos and thus seems perhaps even closer to fabrication, to those contacts with reality which prove ideas, recalling Valéry's dictum that speculation, *savoir*, must finally have an equivalent in *pouvoir*. Unlike Eupalinos, Tridon actually risks his very life with the creations of his mind. He is an adventurer sceptical of moralities, refusing all that is old and familiar, seeking always something new. He is individualistic, self-taught like his creator, infinitely curious, but rejecting mere erudition. And finally, like Valéry himself, this seafarer is an inhabitant of the Mediterranean littoral, 'cette mer Méditer-ranée qui n'a cessé, depuis mon enfance, de m'être présente soit aux yeux, soit à l'esprit' ('Inspirations Méditerranéennes', O.I, p. 1084). His presence in the dialogue completes an evocation of Greece, a country Valéry never visited, but which was important for him because of its architecture, its development of geometry, its philosophers who actually lived their thoughts, and its con-tribution to the creation of modern Europe.

L'AME ET LA DANSE

Writing in 1940 in his *Cahiers* about his feelings of love for several women he had known during his life Valéry said:

Je ne puis absolument pas faire de la littérature avec ces choses-là — ... La litt[érature] pour moi est un moyen *contre* ces poisons imaginaires de tendresse et de jalousie. La litt[érature] ou plutôt, tout ce qui est spirituel, fut toujours mon anti-vie, mon anesthésique. Mais ces sensations cependant furent un puissant excitant intellectuel — le mal exaspérait le remède — *Eupalinos* en 21, *La Danse* en 22, écrits en état de ravage. Et qui le devinerait? (II, pp. 534–5)

The woman in this passage is Catherine Pozzi, with whom Valéry began a liaison in 1920. Their relationship came to an end on 23 October 1921, just three weeks before Valéry finished writing 'L'Ame et la Danse', published in *La Revue Musicale* on 1 December 1921. Although the imagery of the work is often sensual, there are no direct echoes of a love affair in 'L'Ame et la Danse'. It is a delightful Platonic dialogue with a Socrates owing little to Plato, but indebted far more to Valéry, who chose the dialogue form for its great flexibility, and who no doubt valued the characters from Antiquity, Socrates, Phaedrus, and the physician Eryximachus, because of his own Mediterranean origins, and also because they helped create a remoteness from everyday existence. Such distance for Valéry characterized art, and 'L'Ame et la Danse' is a most charming little work of art, derived from those energies noted in the *Cahier* passage above. Valéry himself, in a letter written in 1930, called it a ballet of imagery and ideas:

Quant à la forme d'ensemble, j'ai tenté de faire du *Dialogue* lui-même une manière de ballet dont l'Image et l'Idée sont tour à tour les Coryphées. L'abstrait et le sensible mènent tour à tour et s'unissent enfin dans le vertige.

En somme, je n'ai poursuivi à aucun degré la rigueur historique ou technique (et pour cause). J'ai fait intervenir librement ce qu'il me fallait pour entretenir mon Ballet et en varier les figures. Ceci s'étendit *aux idées mêmes*. Ici elles sont *moyens*. Il est vrai que cette idée (que les idées sont moyens) m'est familière, et peut-être *substantielle*. (O.II, p. 1407)

The dialogue is often poetic, as both Duchesne-Guillemin and Vera Daniel have emphasized, an interplay of sonorities, rhythms, imagery and metaphors.[15] Dramatic and charming images of the dancers mingle with witty exchanges of ideas, ideas about art and the artist, particularly the art of the dance, and ideas about the intellect, about the chilling effects of truth, and about thinking, often an escape from truth, according to Valéry's disabused view of the limits of the mind.

At the same time the dance is seen metaphorically, in sensually elegant evocations by Phaedrus, 'Mille flambeaux, mille péri-styles éphémères, des treilles, des colonnes' (O.II, p. 154), in rigorous intellectual ones by Socrates, who like Valéry in 'Ode Secrète' in *Charmes* compares the dance to movements of the mind. The dance is also action by the body, and Valéry affirmed that a physiological theme ran throughout the dialogue, something recalling the physiological imagery of *La Jeune Parque*, as well as the importance given to the body in 'Eupalinos':

> La pensée constante du *Dialogue* est physiologique, — depuis les troubles digestifs du début prélude, jusqu'à la syncope finale. L'homme est esclave du sympathique et du pn. gastrique. Sensations somptuaires, mouvements de luxe, et pensées spéculatives n'existent qu'à la faveur du bon vouloir de nos tyrans de la vie végétative. La danse est le type de l'échappée. (O.II, p. 1407)

The word 'échappée' here is particularly applicable to the entire ending of the dialogue. Man is a slave of cycles, something the Jeune Parque had already discovered (ll. 260-4), reproductive, digestive, or even intellectual, as in Valéry's *Mon Faust*. Here in 'L'Ame et la Danse', toward the beginning of the dialogue, Socrates describes the cyclical movements of human beings between truth and illusion, thought and dreams, waking and sleeping. Life is a dancer, moving toward one extreme, then the other:

> Elle est une femme qui danse, et qui cesserait divinement d'être femme, si le bond qu'elle a fait, elle y pouvait obéir jusqu'aux nues. Mais comme nous ne pouvons aller à l'infini, ni dans le rêve ni dans la veille, elle, pareillement, redevient toujours elle-même; cesse d'être flocon, oiseau, idée; — d'être enfin tout ce qu'il plut à la flûte qu'elle fût, car la même Terre qui l'a envoyée, la rappelle, et la rend toute haletante à sa nature de femme et à son ami. . . (O.II, p. 151)

This passage anticipates the ending of the dialogue, those final dramatic pages where Athikté's dance is a perfect self-possession, where for a moment she does touch the infinite, escaping from repetition and cycles, thus recalling the Parque's desperate leap toward the Absolute. Here in 'L'Ame et la Danse', the Absolute is reached not through refusal, but through creativity, an artistic act of the body. Valéry, however, contrasts the actions of art with ordinary actions, when Socrates, in the final pages of the dialogue, questions Eryximachus:

Que si nous comparons notre condition pesante et sérieuse à cet état d'étincelante salamandre, ne vous semble-t-il pas que nos actes ordinaires, engendrés successivement par nos besoins, et que nos gestes et nos mouvements accidentels soient comme des matériaux grossiers, comme une impure matière de durée, —tandis que cette exaltation et cette vibration de la vie, tandis que cette suprématie de la tension, et ce ravissement dans le plus agile que l'on puisse obtenir de soi-même, ont les vertus et les puissances de la flamme; et que les hontes, les ennuis, les niaiseries, et les aliments monotones de l'existence s'y consument, faisant briller à nos yeux ce qu'il y a de divin dans une mortelle? (O.II, p. 170)

L'IDEE FIXE OU DEUX HOMMES A LA MER

More than in the other dialogues, there is in this rapid and witty exchange an echo of the eighteenth century, Diderot and Voltaire. There is even a story told within the dialogue, in the manner of *Jacques le Fataliste* (O.II, p. 248), and the various elaborate and absurd titles of books and articles suggested by the interlocutors throughout *L'Idée Fixe* recall 'la métaphysico-théologo-cosmolonigologie' of Pangloss. In an introduction to *L'Idée Fixe*, Valéry explains that the form of the dialogue was a direct result of the lack of time available to him. Since he couldn't develop a few ideas at leisure, he decided upon a lively conversation gliding rapidly from idea to idea, all drawn, as we can now see from his *Cahiers*. A second factor influencing the dialogue is that it was published in an edition destined to be read by members of the French medical profession (O.II, p. 1410), and thus Valéry chose a doctor as his interlocutor. Judith Robinson has suggested that he is Dr Bour, a psychiatrist with whom the Valérys spent a holiday at Agay, on the Riviera.[16] The doctor in the dialogue refers to himself, however, as a general practitioner (O.II, p. 247), and it seems more likely that he is modelled on a number of men in the medical profession whom Valéry knew, although there is no doubt a particular memory of Agay, which Valéry visited in 1931, since the dialogue takes place in a resort on the Mediterranean.

Finally, it is difficult to appreciate fully *L'Idée Fixe* without knowing that it reflects the torments of a love affair with the sculptress Renée Vautier. Valéry refers rather transparently to these sufferings in the first sentence of *L'Idée Fixe*: 'J'étais en proie à de grands tourments; quelques pensées très actives et très aigües me gâtaient tout le reste de l'esprit et du monde' (O.II, p. 197). His obsession with these sufferings even explains the title of the dialogue, as well as the preoccupation throughout with factors limiting or hindering the free functioning of the intellect. Clearly Valéry while writing the dialogue was pondering the phenomenon of frequently recurring mental torture, irrational or 'visceral' reactions to certain images (O.II, p. 224), affectivity (O.II, pp. 217–18), and the mysterious relations between images in the mind and suffering in the body (O.II, p. 217). The functioning memory, which kept bringing back certain past episodes to his mind, is another mystery (O.II, pp. 236–7), and reflection on what was unknowable within himself seems to have developed into a major theme of incomprehension. Man is incapable of completely understanding his body, his inner depths, or 'life', and thus 'ce qu'il y a de plus profond dans l'homme, c'est la peau, – *en tant qu'il se connaît*' (O.II, p. 217). It is perhaps not accidental that *L'Idée Fixe* again and again returns to the theme of automatisms of all kinds, even in modern scientific thinking:

La puissance du moderne est fondée sur 'l'objectivité'. Mais à y regarder de plus près, on trouve que c'est . . . l'objectivité même qui est puissante, — et non l'homme même. Il devient instrument, — esclave — de ce qu'il a trouvé ou forgé: *une manière de voir*. (O.II, p. 253)

Typically, however, throughout *L'Idée Fixe*, Valéry responds to the theme of restrictions with a powerful affirmation of the self.[17] If the mind is limited, usually inattentive and chaotic, and the victim of obsessions, impulses and emotions, Valéry also shows how the mind can orchestrate and develop a number of separate factors (O.II, p. 261), how it is capable of increasing precision (O.II, p. 226), and how it creates order out of disorder (O.II, p. 222 and p. 260). If the objectivity of modern science tends to enslave man, Valéry affirms the possibility of a thinking man. It is his Robinson Crusoe, who appears several times in the dialogue, and who avoids the dangers of imitation and automatism through a measure of intellectual isolation permitting a private world of original thought. It is a world of attention and clarity, preserved from the risks of incoherence. 'La confusion mentale, — qui est plus ou moins pathologique *dans le seul*, — est normale quand on est *plusieurs* . . . L'incohérence, les quiproquos, le coq-à-l'âne, etc., sont de règle, et même de rigueur, dans les conversations, débats, discussions. . .' (O.II, p. 228). Robinson forges his own terminology, and cultivates a certain naiveté and freshness of vision. Thus armed, he cuts through the super-abundance of facts and the narrow perspective of the specialists, and seizes upon the simplest essential terms. He wonders why there is no complete and systematic table of all known human reflexes, why he can find no attempt at a descriptive synthesis of all human functions (O.II, p. 245). He accuses historians of failing to recognize important factors which have determined man's destiny, certain diseases, certain inventions (O.II, p. 210).

This Robinson even disengages his mind from himself, from his accidental and changing personality, to become a pure force of intellectual attention reaching out for new possibilities. Significantly, Valéry's invented word 'implexe' is prominent in *L'Idée Fixe*; it means 'mental capacity', 'mental possibility'. 'Un homme n'est rien tant que rien ne tire de lui des effets ou des productions qui le surprennent . . . en bien, ou en mal. Un homme, à l'état non sollicité est à l'état néant' (O.II, p. 233). As in 'Eupalinos', Valéry presents an intellectual hero toward the end of his dialogue, only here the hero is not mythical, like Tridon, but real: Einstein. Einstein is the counter-thrust to the imprisonment of scientific objectivity and specialization, because he is a truly free and creative mind:

Il se fiait, — en toute conscience, — sachant nettement ce qu'il faisait, — et à quoi il s'exposait . . . à la production par son esprit . . . à la libération de certaines harmonies, sympathies. A l'action ou à l'apparition de certaines préférences, à la suggestion ou perception de certaines symétries, de certaines réponses d'origine obscure, mais assez impérieuses . . . C'est un flair supérieur . . . (O.II, p. 264)

Inevitably we think back to another intellectual hero praised in the final pages of the 'Introduction à la Méthode de Léonard de Vinci' of 1894, who possessed the same intellectual creativity. It was Faraday, who with his imaginative intellect conceived of lines of force in space. Quoting Clerk Maxwell, Valéry wrote:

Faraday voyait, par les yeux de son esprit, des lignes de force traversant tout l'espace où les mathématiciens voyaient des centres de force s'attirant à distance; Faraday voyait un milieu où ils ne voyaient que la distance. (O.I, p. 1195)

MON FAUST

In July 1940, at a time when the future of the human mind as well as that of Europe seemed in grave danger, Paul Valéry began writing *Mon Faust*, composed of two unfinished plays, 'Lust' and 'Le Solitaire'. The two plays, however, reflect in no direct way the anxieties of the war years, no more than did *La Jeune Parque*, written between 1912 and 1917. Instead, the first act of 'Lust' presents a general image of the crisis of twentieth-century science and moral attitudes. Mephistopheles no longer enjoys his former prestige, although he does still have important powers, but only as a symbol of the force of man's instincts. In the second act, a disabused Faust deflates the out-of-date Romantic notions of the Disciple, who believes in inspired genius and glory. The Disciple is used throughout 'Lust' as a foil to Faust, and he again appears in the third act with Mephistopheles in a parody of the old temptation of Faust, announcing to the Devil: 'Je voudrais être grand' (O.II, p. 363). At the same time, this scene, which occurs in Faust's library, serves to develop Valery's ideas on 'non-production', a rejection of the vanities of literary activity in favour of a hidden existence entirely devoted to the study, exercise, and reconstruction of the mind.

It is then perhaps surprising that Faust is writing a book and even dictating it in the course of the play to his attractive young secretary, Lust. This is a book, however, of a very special kind, not to be confused with those in Faust's library. At the very beginning of 'Lust', Faust makes his intentions clear:

Saisissez bien mon dessein général : je puis écrire mes Mémoires . . . Je puis, d'autre part, composer maint traité sur maint sujet. Mais c'est là ce que je ne veux pas faire, et qu'il m'ennuierait de faire. Et puis, je trouve que c'est une manière de falsification que de séparer la pensée, même la plus abstraite, de la vie, même la plus . . . vécue . . . Donc, j'ai résolu d'insérer purement et simplement, comme elles me vinrent, mes observations, mes spéculations, mes thèses, mes idées, dans le récit assez merveilleux de ce qui m'est advenu, et de mes rapports avec les hommes et les choses . . . (O.II, p. 281)

What Faust is writing then is not a book in the usual sense of the word, but a revelation of the functioning thinker seen in his entirety. When completed, these notes will exhaust for Faust all the possibilities of his mind, 'toutes mes voix diverses', 'vrais et faux souvenirs', what he actually did and what he might have done, and 'celui qui l'aura lu n'en pourra plus lire d'autre' (O.II, p. 297). The result of this exhaustion will be a complete freeing of the mind, beyond the cycles and repetitiveness to which a second existence had condemned Faust, and which already plagued Monsieur Teste in 1894,[18] and the heroine of Valéry's great poem, *La Jeune Parque*,[19] as well as their creator, Valéry himself.[20] Once liberated, a Faust completely detached from his person and existence will face death 'comme un voyageur qui a fait abandon de son bagage et marche à l'aventure, sans souci de ce qu'il laisse après soi' (O.II, p. 299). The ending of 'Le Solitaire' reveals a very similar attitude, when Faust refuses the offer of yet another life: 'J'en sais trop pour aimer, j'en sais trop pour haïr / Et je suis excédé d'être une créature.' (O.II, p. 402). Both attitudes reflect the objective of Valéry's entire existence, expressed already in the 'Que peut un homme?' of Monsieur Teste, and finally in the last notes of the last *Cahier*:

La mort est très rarement autre chose qu'une interruption définitive — Peut-être toujours. On peut cependant concevoir des cas où elle soit 'naturelle' — c'est-à-dire *par épuisement (relatif) des combinaisons d'une vie*. C'était mon idée p[our] le dialogue (*Perì tôn tôn Theôn*).

— Quant à moi, *jusqu'au bout* fut mon désir 1. en fait d'*intellect* — arriver par manœuvres et exercices d'imagination et self-conscience à former l'idée de nos possibilités — d'où épuisement des philosophies — par *voie de possession des formes* et transformations, le *groupe des notions*, 2. en fait d'affectivité — sensibilités a) sensorielles — b) AMOUR. (I, p. 231)

'Le Solitaire' reveals still another ending for an intellectual life in the very strange character of the Solitaire himself, who lives on the peak of a cold and barren mountain, symbol of the same liberation sought by Faust. The Solitaire, however, who has presumably exhausted all the possibilities of the mind, has concluded by destroying that mind itself, and he reflects one of Valéry's essential myths, his 'Caligulism': 'En somme — Je cherchais à me posséder — Et voilà mon mythe — — à me posséder . . . pour me détruire — je veux dire pour *être une fois pour toutes*' (*Cahiers*, I, p. 183).

But before Faust's conclusion by exhaustion of possibilities, liberation, and death, there is in 'Lust' a remarkable apotheosis of *life* in the garden-scene of the second act. Here the magical, musical spell of a beautiful evening brings Faust rapidly to a high point of pure enjoyment of being. A sense of *extreme* existence embraces the whole man, mind, body and sensibility. Already in 1919 in 'Note et Digression', Valéry had stressed Leonardo's appreciation of the human body (O.I, p. 1214), although it was the dialogue 'Eupalinos' in 1921 which gave it major importance in the famous 'prayer to the body' (O.II, pp. 99–100). 'Lust', however, is the first published work which attempts to synthesize extreme existence of mind and body with the extreme experience of love, even if in a very incomplete fashion. Almost from the beginning of the garden-scene Lust shows her love for Faust, and immediately after Faust's great monologue, she unconsciously places her hand upon his shoulder. Faust addresses her as 'tu' and there is a brief moment of emotional communion with a birth of intimacy and tenderness, those beginnings of love which Valéry prized above all other joys.[21] Immediately, however, Faust retreats, and the apotheosis of the garden-scene comes to an end as he turns again to the dictation of his memoirs.

Valéry planned a fourth act for 'Lust' which would have developed the love theme, but he found the project too difficult for theatrical creation, perhaps in large part because of his own defensive attitudes. Already in the first act, Faust tells Mephistopheles that he wants only tenderness, not love, from Lust: 'Point d'amour: je sais trop qu'il s'achève en ruine, en dégoût, en désastres: c'est le froid, c'est la haine, ou la mort qui termine ces jeux de la chair ou du cœur, et qui règle leur compte aux délices!' (O.II, p. 293). The monstrous Goungoune and his master Mephistopheles both have the power to create erotic dreams, and Lust, who represents the emotional and spontaneous side of man, while Faust symbolizes lucidity and self-awareness, has already been a victim of one of these dreams, as we discover at the end of the first act. Love is a danger because so closely related to instincts, to the cyclical and repetitive functions of life. There are echoes of Valéry's past in this defensiveness, echoes of the Serpent and erotic dream which begin *La Jeune Parque*, and also of his personal experiences of love. His liaison with Catherine Pozzi in 1920 ended painfully and abruptly in October 1921, and was already reflected in the second section of the 'Fragments du Narcisse' of *Charmes*, while the torments of his affair with Renée Vautier had some influence on *L'Idée Fixe*. And so the intimacy of Lust and Faust is only a fleeting moment in the second act, and the too difficult fourth act was never written. Five years after beginning *Mon Faust*, and a few weeks before his death, Valéry wrote in his *Cahiers*: 'Lust et Faust sont *moi* — et rien que moi. L'expérience m'a montré que ce que j'ai le plus désiré ne se trouve pas dans l'autrui — et ne peut trouver *l'autre* capable de tenter sans réserve l'essai d'aller jusqu'au bout dans la volonté de. . . *porter l'amour où il n'a jamais été*' (II, p. 556).

V

VALERY AND THE MODERN WORLD

Between the two world wars, and increasingly after 1930, Valéry turned his attention to the political, social and economic problems of the century, although as early as 1895 and 1898 he had shown a remarkable sensitivity to the significance of the emergence of Japan and the United States as world powers, and in late 1896 he wrote the prescient article 'La Conquête Allemande' (later titled 'Une Conquête Méthodique', O.I, pp. 971–87) with its brilliant analysis of modern totalitarianism. He chose to remain aloof from the problems he examined, viewing them from a distance, and he has been criticized for his refusal of 'engagement'. There is, however, a good deal to be said in defence of Valéry's attitude. Obviously he wished to choose a position which would most protect and favour the free operation of the critical intellect, and he well understood the opposition between intellectual liberty and involvement in politics. In 'La Liberté de l'Esprit' (O.II, pp. 1077–99), he argues that politics is necessarily concerned with the attainment and conservation of power, causing politicians and those closely linked to politics to twist the truth. Valéry wanted to preserve intellectual calm, purity and objectivity in the study of complex problems which seemed to require just those qualities of mind. He gives as an example of such problems, in 'Lettre sur la Société des Esprits' (O.I, pp. 1138–1146), the gap which the twentieth century had created between the recent discoveries of modern science and age-old prejudices, attitudes, habits of mind. Valéry was well aware that the findings of modern psychology, for instance, conflicted with received ideas about such things as free will and responsibility. Here was just one opportunity for a detached and informed mind, with no axe to grind, to make a contribution to general awareness, and it so happens that in his *Cahiers*, Valéry frequently turned to the question of free will. Another problem might be the true interests of a nation in the increasingly complex world of modern times. 'Rien ne me paraît plus difficile que de déterminer les vrais intérêts d'une nation, qu'il ne faut pas confondre avec ses vœux'

(O.II, p. 931). Not only was Valéry unwilling to leave such problems to politicians, he was unwilling also to leave them to 'specialists', since one of his fundamental convictions was that a mind with a broad general perspective can furnish insights which escape the specialists. Where Valéry can be faulted is in his excessive hopes that intellectual analysis might play an important role in the choice and formulation of policy. True, he could at times sound like Jean-Paul Sartre, noting that policy choices are essentially derived from irrational attitudes and that tensions in society are inevitable, never to be erased by reasoning: 'Il n'y aurait de paix véritable que si tout le monde était satisfait' (O.II, p. 931). But the temptation of the intellect was such that he too often yielded to the Western rationalist tradition: '*Si nous avions plus d'esprit, et si nous donnions à l'esprit plus de place et plus de pouvoir véritable dans les choses de ce monde, ce monde aurait plus de chances de se rétablir, et plus promptement*' (O.I, p. 1139) (Valéry's italics).

When it came to analysing the modern world, however, Valéry's intellect produced lucid views of its fundamental aspects, in part because he always strove to free himself from influences of the past in order to determine what was truly *new*. Typically, after the fall of France in May 1940, Valéry, unlike the Vichy government, refused to preoccupy himself with past events and guilts, and preferred to think of the future and its problems. Valéry was sceptical of studies of the past, of history, which he viewed as merely hypotheses, and particularly of the 'lessons of history', of the ability of past experience to foresee the future. Any such prediction in the period following the first world war had already seemed to him particularly hazardous because so many things had changed so quickly and so radically. Like a number of his perceptive contemporaries, Valéry was well aware that the post-war world was in a state of crisis, a crisis of beliefs, of morality and religion, of international politics, even of science. His famous essay, 'La Crise de l'Esprit' (O.I, pp. 988–1014) of 1919, dwelt on the cœxistence in the modern mind of *opposed* ideas and attitudes, and emphasized the transience of beliefs: 'Personne ne peut dire ce qui demain sera mort ou vivant en littérature, en philosophie, en esthétique' (O.I, p. 990). Traditional morality and religion had been shaken. Valéry remarked on the disappearance of such old terms as 'vertu', 'homme de bien', 'honneur', and realized also that modern psychology was profoundly affecting morality, that modern science had dethroned religion, although without giving modern man a new sense of his justification. Science, of course, had created modern warfare: 'Nous avons vu, de nos yeux vu, le travail consciencieux, l'instruction la plus solide, la discipline et l'application les plus sérieuses, adaptés à d'épouvantables desseins' (O.I, p. 989). Scientific progress, making increasing demands on sources of energy and raw materials, was polluting the air man breathed (O.II, p. 1061), while giving him immense powers to which he had difficulty adapting, moving man further and further away from the simple conditions of life. Here are the first lines of 'Notre Destin et les Lettres', written in 1937:

L'esprit a transformé le monde et le monde le lui rend bien. Il a mené l'homme où il ne savait point aller. Il nous a donné le goût et les moyens de vivre, il nous a conféré un pouvoir d'action qui dépasse énormément les forces d'adaptation, et même la capacité de compréhension des individus; il nous a inspiré des désirs et obtenu des résultats qui excèdent de beaucoup ce qui est utile à la vie. (O.II, p. 1059)

It is to Valéry's credit that he saw the emphasis on method, organization, and positive thinking in modern science as potential threats to genuine liberty of the intellect:

La puissance du moderne est fondée sur 'l'objectivité'. Mais à y regarder de plus près, on trouve que c'est . . . l'objectivité même qui est puissante, — et non l'homme même. Il devient instrument, — esclave, — de ce qu'il a trouvé ou forgé: *une manière de voir*. (O.II, p. 253)

Europe had created modern science and modern technology, and Valéry wrote often of the accomplishments of Europe, of the influence of the Mediterranean on its development, of its origins in Greece, Rome and Christianity. He was equally aware of European activities and influences in the non-European world, and of the consequent threat to the importance of Europe. Not only was Europe dangerously weakened by the first world war, but it had also exported its technology to new and emerging nations all over the earth, thus creating economic rivalry and the possibility of its own decline:

Considérez un peu ce qu'il adviendra de l'Europe quand il existera par ses soins, en Asie, deux douzaines de Creusot ou d'Essen, de Manchester, ou de Roubaix, quand l'acier, la soie, le papier, les produits chimiques, les étoffes, la céramique et le reste y seront produits en quantités écrasantes, à des prix invincibles. (O.II, p. 927)

Instead of uniting to be strong and to maintain the importance of Europe, European countries, through nationalism and old rivalries, were further weakening its position in the world. 'Il n'y aura rien eu de plus sot dans toute l'histoire que la concurrence européenne en matière politique et économique, comparée, combinée et confrontée avec l'unité et l'alliance européenne en matière scientifique' (O.II, p. 926). Valéry asks then his famous question: 'L'Europe deviendra-t-elle *ce qu'elle est en réalité*, c'est-à-dire: un petit cap du continent asiatique?' (O.I, p. 995).

At the same time that far-off nations were modernizing themselves with European technology, international communications had become so rapid that no important events could be localized any more, and their effects became incalculable:

Les *effets des effets*, qui étaient autrefois insensibles ou négligeables relativement à la durée d'une vie humaine, et à l'aire d'action d'un pouvoir humain, se font sentir presque instantanément à toute distance, reviennent aussitôt vers leurs causes, ne s'amortissent que dans l'imprévu.

(O.II, p. 924)

Thus we find Valéry passionately interested in international understanding and international cooperation, critical of the tendency toward autarchy which seemed to him so opposed to the facts of modern life. In 1928 he remarks: 'Il serait bien pénible et presque impossible de duper, de vexer ou de supprimer quelqu'un dont la vie profonde vous serait présente et la sensibilité mesurable par la vôtre' (O.II, p. 1033). International understanding would favour the chances of world peace, while an acquaintance with foreign cultures would be an enrichment for Europe, just as the meeting of many cultures along the shores of the Mediterranean had been a vivifying influence in the past. In an analogous way Valéry spoke of the benefits he gained at meetings of the *Académie Française*, where important men of many different occupations, philosophers, poets, historians, diplomats met and talked. Once again there is a manifestation of his reluctance to remain within a narrow specialization, and of his taste for universality and the new perspectives it affords.

This brings us back to a consideration of the individual and of what is best for the individual intellect, no doubt Valéry's most important preoccupation in his study and critique of the twentieth century, and his most important message for men of today. He fully realized that work in the modern world tended toward specialization and that specializations were in turn controlled by organization, and he feared the stifling effect of these factors and regretted the disappearance of the 'complete man' now being replaced by collaboration, team efforts, hierarchies, vast systems. Modern work at its worst, of course, was factory production where each worker repeats endlessly one small task. 'Mais combien de métiers se réduisent à un automatisme, et lui sacrifient peu à peu ce qu'il y a dans l'homme de plus précieux!' (O.II, p. 1110). In such situations, all the precious advantages to be gained from confronting problems, solving difficulties, struggling, and expending effort are lost, and Valéry never ceased believing in the virtue of effort: 'Je ne crains pas les épines! / L'éveil est bon, même dur!' ('Aurore', ll. 71–2, *Charmes*). At the same time, there is a disappearance of the leisure needed for solving difficulties; rapidity is prized above all things, and man is tyrannized and harassed by timetables, production schedules, competition. Already in 1935 Valéry noted that insomnia and the consumption of sleeping pills were becoming widespread!

Thus we have a situation in the twentieth century where very frequently work does not serve to enrich the individual, and then neither does his free time. Valéry saw the mind of man attacked on all sides by modern means of communication, by political parties and their propaganda, by the press and by advertising:

L'homme moderne est l'esclave de la modernité: il n'est point de progrès qui ne tourne à sa plus complète servitude. Le confort nous enchaîne. La liberté de la presse et les moyens trop puissants dont elle dispose nous assassinent de clameurs imprimées, nous percent de nouvelles à sensations. La publicité, un des plus grands maux de ce temps, insulte nos regards, falsifie toutes les épithètes, gâte les paysages, corrompt toute qualité et toute critique . . . (O.II, p. 968).

These assaults on the intellect produce habits of conformity, the sterility of imitation, and 'ideas' which really aren't ideas at all, but instead the mere parroting of notions absorbed from the milieu:

Nous répondrons le plus souvent à ce qui nous frappe par des paroles dont nous ne sommes pas les véritables auteurs. Notre pensée — ou ce que nous prenons pour notre pensée — n'est alors qu'une simple réponse automatique. C'est pourquoi il faut difficilement se croire soi-même *sur parole.* Je veux dire que la parole qui nous vient à l'esprit, générale-ment n'est pas de nous. (O.I, p. 1080)

This impoverished man is only a cog in the bureaucratic modern state, manipulated and constrained at every turn. From such a political democracy there can be an easy passage to tyrannical centralized power, resulting in a further deprivation of liberty and a further degradation of intellect. In 1939, Valéry had this to say about Nazi Germany:

Du côté de nos ennemis, nous savons (et le monde entier) que toute leur politique à l'égard de l'esprit s'est réduite ou acharnée depuis dix ans, à réprimer les développements de l'intelligence, à déprécier les valeurs de la recherche pure, à prendre des mesures, souvent atroces, contre ceux qui s'y consacraient, à favoriser, jusque dans les chaires ou aux laboratoires, les adorateurs de l'idole au détriment des créateurs indépendants de richesse spirituelle, et à imposer aux arts comme aux sciences, les fins utilitaires que poursuit un pouvoir fondé sur les déclamations et sur la terreur. Les universités, jadis la plus grande et la plus juste gloire de leur pays, ont été privées des meilleurs de leurs maîtres, soumises au contrôle d'un parti qui est une police; leurs étudiants transformés en satellites du régime ou en ouvriers enrégimentés; enfin, la doctrine de l'Etat s'est, là-bas, nettement et brutalement prononcée contre l'intégrité et la dignité de la pensée qui ne doit s'employer qu'à le servir. (O.II, p. 1117)

And so on one hand there was the 'pure poet' and the detached thinker who refused 'engagement', and who felt so disgusted at times with French democracy that he would dream of a state ruled by method and order. On the other hand, there was the Valéry so profoundly concerned with the integrity of the indi-vidual that he never yielded to the temptation of a dictatorial regime, but instead attacked the totalitarian powers in the thirties, opposed Vichy and his old friend Marshal Pétain, and then reacted with extraordinary equanimity in a time of passions and pressures, when after the liberation of Paris he intervened to obtain mercy for the collaborators Maurras, Brasillach and Bérard. A passage from Valéry's December 1944 discourse honouring Voltaire reveals the sureness of his instincts:

Il fait comprendre aussi que le châtiment quelquefois se fait lui-même crime, car le spectacle d'épouvantables supplices réveille et entretient la férocité latente des uns, tandis qu'il transforme aux yeux des autres, en presque innocente victime, celui qui n'était qu'un misérable criminel. Si la puissance publique se passionne, qu'elle s'acharne sur un corps de coupable, si elle épouse la colère ou poursuit une sorte de vengeance, la notion abstraite et pure de l'Etat rendant la justice en est altérée et dégradée. On s'avise que l'Etat lui-même est exercé par des instincts qu'il ne devrait pas connaître, et qu'il ne connaît qu'aux dépens de sa raison d'être même. (O.I, p. 526)

VI

CAHIERS

Every day between 1894 and 1945, Valéry rose at 4.00 a.m. and for three or four hours made notes of ideas which came to his mind. This was in no way the usual private diary, but instead a meditation on thoughts related to Valéry's major preoccupation: the functioning of the human mind. By the end of his life, Valéry had filled 261 notebooks, and had made two attempts at classifying all these ideas. A first classification was begun in 1908 and a second planned in 1921. In 1922, Valéry had the services of the first of a number of secretaries who typed his ideas on separate sheets of paper. Beginning in the 1930s, Valéry himself, aided by a number of people, classified this material. Often he made annotations or additions to what he had previously written.

Between 1957 and 1961, the Centre National de la Recherche Scientifique made a photographic copy of the original notebooks which were published in 29 volumes, nearly 29,600 pages. Then, when the classified dossiers were discovered, a new edition in two volumes was published in 1972–4 by the Bibliothèque de la Pléiade, edited by Judith Robinson, which followed Valéry's own classifications. We have based our introduction to the *Cahiers* on this edition, omitting only the sections 'Poïétique', 'Poésie', and 'Poèmes et PPA [Petits Poèmes Abstraits]'. The first two are utilized in our chapter on Valéry's poetics and the last one did not lend itself to any reasonable treatment in the format we have adopted: a presentation of the major ideas of the various sections of the *Cahiers*.

CAHIERS: VOLUME I

Les Cahiers

This section shows that the *Cahier* notes were considered by Valéry to be tentative explorations of the human mind intended for his own intellectual 'self-reconstruction'. They were private notes written for himself, although two notes here do contemplate eventual publication (p. 5, p. 10). (Fragments from the *Cahiers* were published during Valéry's lifetime.) It is the organization of this material, however, which preoccupies him far more than any thought of publication (p. 8, p. 14).

Ego

One of the major themes of this section is Valéry's detachment, from, for example, demands of the body and his powerful emotions (p. 106). Yet on p. 53 his attitude toward emotions is ambiguous when he describes a certain contralto voice which pressed in him the 'mamelles sacrées / ignobles / de l'émotion / bête / . . .' The wariness toward emotions is part of a larger refusal of all the repeated and trivial exigencies of 'life' (p. 176). Valéry appreciates 'inhumanity' and not the echoes of banal existence in the works of man (p. 117), and although he is sociable, he is not social, an intellectual Robinson Crusoe. 'Ne me servir que d'idées que j'ai forgées' (p. 26). If he discovers that others share *his* ideas, he fears that he is no longer exploring what is new and undiscovered. Rather than absorbing the contents of books written by others, he picks out ideas which will stimulate his own mind.

Fleeing the particularity of his own person, his memories, his past, even his own ideas and any form of intellectual specialization, Valéry prefers the universality of the *Moi Pur*, 'un certain regard qui rend *toutes choses égales*' (p. 121), and his major moral principle is to increase his intellectual powers (p. 23). His method seeks first of all a freshness of vision. 'Ma faculté – voir facilement les choses comme dénuées de *sens*' (p. 32). He focusses his mind on the essential aspects of a problem (p. 187), and then seeks multiple perspectives or else enlarges his perspective to include a wider context (p. 115). His mind is rapid, working quickly and then abandoning an idea to return to it later (p. 59). Similarly, he observes a larger cyclical movement in his intellectual pre-occupations (pp. 55–6, p. 84). At all times he demands effort from his mind (p. 124), rigour (p. 28), and critical awareness (p. 102), highly sceptical of anything merely spontaneous (p. 182). In his solutions he likes to tend toward constructions, toward 'l'expéri-ence précise' (p. 106).

Once the problem is solved, he pushes on to something else (p. 132), refusing even to proselytize others because he is always so aware of the limits and defects of the human mind. From his keen awareness of these limits he even imagines that he derives a special strength (p. 33). Finally, the production of works is not his objective, but instead a knowledge of the functioning of the mind and an increase of its powers (p. 21). At times he imagines reaching an extreme of self-possession where the next step would be self-destruction. This is Valéry's famous 'Caligulisme', described here in two passages (p. 183 and p. 226).

Ego Scriptor

Several times in this section Valéry mentions his admiration for music and architecture, privileged arts which construct their compositions out of pure formal elements (p. 274). He constantly stressed the importance of form in poetry, elaborating the conditions governing a work before attempting to find the words, then creating a construction with liaisons and correspondences between its parts (p. 295), moving from the merely arbitrary to true necessity. He criticized the novel, because he felt it never reached any necessity of form.

Literature for Valéry was essentially a 'spéculation linguistique' (p. 241), and in 1924 he wrote that he could no longer write poetry (after a very productive period) because he had crossed through 'une zone de *mots*' (p. 257). Literature for Valéry was not a pseudo-reality, a fantasy, or a reflection of the real life of the author intended to excite the reader. Its language should be impersonal and universal, purified of personal allusion, a special language, divorced from everyday reality and 'formes toutes faites' (p. 235). Valéry felt that his self-training in mathematics had given him the necessary intellectual rigour to create that special language (p. 248). The purpose of this language was to enchant the reader (p. 318). Valéry would have liked the effects of this language to emerge entirely from the intentions of the poet (p. 259), but this is impossible. He responds to this impossibility, however, by again affirming the all-importance of form (p. 295).

In the same year (1939) that he makes this affirmation, however, he distinguishes himself from Mallarmé, for whom language and form were paramount, and claims that for him what 'speaks' in a poem is not language but the sensibility of the functioning, living and thinking human being (p. 293, see also p. 298). A somewhat similar idea had occurred as early as 1900 (p. 235). In late 1907 Valéry had noted that an interest in form had led him toward an indifference to content and thus to an interest in the functioning mind itself (p. 239). His preoccupation with function had convinced him that literature was a waste of time and poetry often seemed to him an incomplete mental activity (p. 256, p. 279). In 1910 he wrote: 'L'habitude de méditer chasse enfin le pouvoir et la manie d'écrire', although admitting that clarity of thought emerges from 'la volonté d'écrire ou fixer' (p. 240). So poetry became subservient to the objective of training and investigating the intellect, and the famous word 'exercise' is applied to poetry as early as 1905 (p. 238). All literary activity for Valéry had to imply hard thinking and mental transformations and he simply rejected anything 'given', such as descriptions (p. 309). He liked to begin with little information, using it to stimulate his mind to further activity (p. 283), and the final aim of his literary activity was an elaboration of the self. 'Ce travail . . . ne fut qu'une élaboration indéfiniment entretenue de moi-même' (p. 300).

Gladiator

The title of this section is the name of a famous racehorse, and implies a training of the mind. Valéry was not interested in the products of the mind, but in its processes. His ambition was neither to know everything nor to be a superhuman intellect, but to realize completely the possibilities of the mind he had. 'Il n'y a qu'une chose à faire: se refaire. Ce n'est pas simple' (p. 342). This is what he implied by 'orgueil', which he prized, while disdaining 'vanité' and 'amour-propre' (p. 353).

Logic is only a part of the art of thinking, best developed by poetry, mathematics and drawing, and best assisted by a number of disciplines rather than specialization (p. 337). This art of thinking embraces not only one's intellectual powers but also one's weaknesses. The conscious mind and the unconscious mind depend on each other (pp. 336 and 369). Thinking should begin with a naivety of vision at what Valéry calls the 'zero-point' (pp. 358 and 372). The thinker must above all know the right questions (p. 364) and he must operate with an economy of time and actions so as to maximize intellectual liberty. Conclusions must be verified by proofs. Valéry was sceptical of unverified thinking (p. 376). Once something is verified, it is discarded, and Valéry pushes on to something new (p. 367).

Langage

Valéry emphasizes that languages were created historically, in response to specific needs. Thus words were formed to designate isolated objects or phenomena and not for linking objects and phenomena. The mind using a language today is organized historically, imitatively, by that language. Of itself, a language determines things, generalizes things in the mind (p. 383). The expression 'la vie et la mort' creates a false idea of opposition whereas one of these phenomena needs the other. Anthropomorphic tendencies in language create such expressions as 'Dieu' and 'Nature'. Language gives us problems and answers which aren't ours. Our fundamental ideas are thus inherited and unexamined (p. 406).

Valéry attacks a verbalism which replaces true observation and thought. Some even wish to explore words, hoping thus to discover a new knowledge. 'Travailler sérieusement sur ces mots c'est attribuer à cette formation géologique accidentée les propriétés d'une architecture' (p. 436). Many can think only in the form of given words and what cannot be expressed simply doesn't exist for them. Valéry makes the interesting remark that those who think only in words have no style. 'Le style naît de la netteté de la pensée s'opposant à l'insuffisance, à l'inertie, au vague *moyen* du langage et le violant avec bonheur' (p. 403).

The problem of language is that it represents a relatively continuous series with a collection of finite elements (p. 384). Reality is far too complex for language (p. 386). We must learn to think without language, but there are limits to this thinking. If language is eliminated, thinking degenerates into mere dreams. Thus man needs language in order to think and a precise language, a project never entirely realized. 'Mon projet primitif – de me faire un langage propre – je n'ai pu le pousser. Il ne m'en est resté que l'abstention de bien des mots (quand je pense *pour moi*) et l'habitude de ne tenir les paroles que pour des expédients individuels' (p. 428).

Philosophie

In an early *Cahier* Valéry wrote a paragraph making three attacks on philosophers, on systematic doubt, on bad questions and on unprovable answers (p. 517). Since philosophy doesn't correspond to reality it should be considered to be a 'form' of all that the philosopher knows. If the form is pleasing, it becomes *art* (p. 665). Even logic has little or no relation with reality, since it is often only a structure based on conventions (p. 666). Valéry criticizes Spinoza, Bergson, Oriental philosophy, even Kant. Nietzsche is admired, but also ridiculed for his pretentiousness and foolish ideas.[1] Only Descartes receives fulsome praise, for his precise, methodical and verifiable thought (p. 601).

Valéry points out that the *Cogito* means nothing, but is important as an affirmation of the self as judge of evidence. Valéry too begins with a *table rase* (p. 660), and begins also with sense data from a real world which he refuses to doubt (pp. 489, 560, 728). Metaphysics is totally rejected (pp. 519, 709, 557, 492, 602). We need an attentive observation of reality and a scrupulous attention to language (p. 517). Valéry criticizes philosophers for talking of 'movement' without knowing what it is (p. 541). The same criticism is applied to Bergson's discussion of 'liberty' (p. 663). Another note reminds us that *'matière et esprit* sont des mots' (p. 708), and 'toute la question de la réalité, célèbre en philosophie, provient de la valeur abusive donnée au mot: *réalité'* (p. 656). Repeatedly Valéry attacks philosophers who hope to obtain answers by interrogating isolated words. He points out that a word needs at least a sentence around it to begin limiting its meanings (p. 586). Again and again he returns to Zeno's famous paradoxes to show the gap between the philosopher's use of language and the world of reality (p. 556).

It is important to ask the right questions of reality, and first of all to study 'natural' problems, not those artificially generated or created by language. These problems must be precise and limited (p. 482), have possible answers (p. 559) and escape anthropomorphic influences. Valéry sees anthropomorphic biases as an inevitable determinism influencing our reasoning. He is, however, no determinist, realizing with modern science that causality is highly complex (p. 512). But he seems to be no apostle of 'free will' either. He finds the idea of free will difficult to define, suggests that it depends no doubt on the time available for a reaction (p. 721), and emphasizes that the past limits human choices (p. 509). One such constraint is the structure of language itself which shapes our thinking (p. 730). Another is the anthropomorphism of the 'conscious voluntary action' which creates in man the questions *why*, *who*, *when*, and these questions have in turn produced metaphysics (p. 711). Still another anthropomorphic determinism is created by man's æsthetic sensibility which tends to create symmetries: good and evil, matter and spirit, vice and virtue (p. 674).

Valéry's method will avoid anthropomorphic influences and will try to ask the right questions with a precise language while obtaining sense data from an attentive observation of reality. All this process depends on an even more essential philosophy of *self-awareness* (p. 625). *Conscience de soi* never forgets that thinking can *never* be the equivalent of reality (p. 505). *Conscience de soi* and awareness of mental imagery as such are really the cornerstones of Valéry's philosophy (p. 604). If thinking is not the equivalent of reality, man at any one time will have only a perspective on reality, a partial truth formed by the observer and the real world. Thus it is important to multiply perspectives (p. 494). Knowledge can never be exhaustive, but is always progressive, and a 'system' is thus excluded (p. 625). Instead of creating a 'system', the modern thinker attempts to verify progressive knowledge. Valéry is no speculating, theorizing mind of the ivory tower, but a down-to-earth realist, a modern Voltaire (p. 701).

Système

Valéry was dissatisfied with the available terminology for describing the operations of the brain (pp. 807, 809) and he hoped for a new language and symbols modelled on the example of mathematical physics. One of his important ideas was that rather than attempting an exhaustive explanation of the brain, it would be better to *represent* its functioning with models, and thus Valéry anticipates modern cybernetics (p. 855). His specific intentions were to protect his mind against its own thoughts and feelings by being aware of their relative value, and then to train his mind, increase its powers and push to the limit of its capacities (pp. 793, 822). He realized, however, that he was not creating a science of the mind, but instead his own personal theories, useful for himself and perhaps not for others (p. 821).

The basic law of Valéry's intellectual functioning was 'self-variance', or the tendency of the mind constantly to change the object of its attention (p. 861). The number of ideas the mind could entertain at one time was also limited, and this group of ideas depended entirely on the 'phase', by which Valéry meant a certain organization of the mind (e.g. to produce poetry). The 'phase' requires a certain 'montage', and passages from phase to phase are more or less rapid. Within each phase, Valéry used the term 'act' to unify the mind's operation. Essentially the 'act' follows a 'demand-response' pattern, a cyclical evolution comparable to a thermodynamic cycle and moving from availability to specialization (which Valéry calls 'écart') and back to availability. The laws governing transforming and conserving functions were called by Valéry 'N plus S' or 'nombres plus subtils' (p. 850). He was aware, however, that the continuous form of geometric analysis was not adequate to describe the discontinuous movements of the mind (p. 837). As early as 1917 he was aware of the problem: 'L'incessante arrivée des sensations, la prodigieuse et perpétuelle activité des associations, cela met en jeu des nombres énormes. Les lois font banqueroute dans ce chaos' (p. 801).

Psychologie

Valéry was well aware of the all-important role of the senses and the sensibility in the creation of thought (pp. 897, 1115). The mind's conscious potential response to activation of the sensibility is a large part of what Valéry means by the term 'implexe', which plays such an important role in *L'Idée Fixe* (O.II, pp. 195–275) and which Valéry defines at length in this section of the *Cahiers* (p. 1081). Other activities of the mind imply little or no conscious functioning: laughter (p. 904), tears (895), instinctive acts (p. 1023), intuitions (p. 1031), and automatism (988). A mental 'phase', which is a special organization of the mind oriented in a certain direction, groups conscious and unconscious operations and is characterized by the collaboration of a 'group' of 'functions' (p. 968). Surprise indicates the inadequacy of a phase faced with a demand it can't process. If the phase is adequate, however, the mind furnishes responses and there is an excursion away from indifference (p. 1061). This excursion is marked by increasing attention, which Valéry compares to an eye adjusting itself to an object (p. 1021), and all depends on the amount of time available (p. 879). The adjustments resulting from growing attention show that there is no such thing as an *isolated* idea in the mind. An idea is attached to a sensation, to related ideas, to what precedes and follows it (p. 921). The mind is a transforming agent, constantly changing, but also conserving (pp. 882, 1032, 1073). It is not imagined by Valéry as a mechanical operation, but as an energy system (p. 970). Valéry gave the name 'nombres plus subtils' to the laws of transformation and conservation (p. 1090). But it would be difficult to express these laws since chance intervenes so much (p. 939).

These operations are limited by many factors and Valéry devoted much study to the limits of the intellect, attempting to know them, and if possible transcend them (p. 998). As in *La Jeune Parque*, he was most aware here of the relation between functions of the body and the mind. 'Trouver dans la pensée et dans les produits de la pensée les traces, les caractères du fonctionnement de l'être vivant. Ce qui donne des limites et des conditions à cette pensée' (p. 975). Looking at man from an organic point of view, Valéry considers him as a higher form of animal, but he carefully distinguishes man from animal. Man can enumerate and contemplate various possibilities (p. 1055). He also chooses (p. 998), and to choose he divides the mind into two parts, image and attention (p. 990). Valéry would like the image of the exterior world scrutinized by attention always to appear new and original, recalling his discussion of observation in 'Introduction à la Méthode de Léonard de Vinci' (O.I, p. 1165) (p. 1039). But Valéry realizes also that thinking is impossible without sameness, or conservation (p. 1040). This conservation, however, doesn't imply that the mind repeats itself. On the contrary, the mind rejects repetition (p. 983). It also rejects many other thoughts, those without utility (pp. 914, 1054). When it is transforming a 'useful' idea, it moves toward an objective, an optimum, a *seuil*, through trial and error or by the addition of acts, and then relaxes and returns to a neutral position (p. 937). But the mind is not long neutral, because there is no such thing as a 'final thought' (p. 933). Valéry pondered the question of what remained constant and invariant in this constantly changing functioning: 'Question capitale de *ma* pyschologie. Qu'est-ce qui se conserve à travers tous les états? qu'est-ce qui se conserve dans le sommeil, le rêve, l'ivresse, l'épouvante, la fureur de l'amour? la démence?' (pp. 965–6).

Soma et C.E.M.

'C.E.M.' stands for 'corps, esprit, monde' and is an important concept for Valéry: 'Les 3 dim[ensions] de la connaissance. Le corps, le monde, l'esprit. – Cette division *simpliste* est pourtant capitale. Elle est cachée dans toute connaissance' (p. 1126). Valéry theorizes that it is the 'insufficiency' of the world about us which stimulates our feelings, thoughts and acts, and the mind in turn fosters this impression of insufficiency (p. 1131). The importance of the body in the thinking process cannot be overemphasized (pp. 1120, 1126), although the body is a mystery for the intellect (p. 1119). Man functions very well, however, without detailed knowledge of his body (p. 1122), and, in fact, constant detailed knowledge of his body would hamper his functioning (p. 1137).

Sensibilité

Valéry considered sensibility the most essential intellectual function: 'La sensibilité est le fait le plus important de tous – il les englobe tous, est omniprésent et omni-constituant. Ce qu'on appelle *connaissance* n'est qu'une complication de ce fait' (p. 1197). He distinguishes himself from the sensualists however, because for Valéry sense data are only the beginning of the cognitive process (p. 1166). The mind is stimulated by the sensibility, stimulus which Valéry calls an 'inégalité', a 'manque', or an attribution of 'valeurs'. A man may find, for example, that the world is not beautiful enough, and so he creates a painting (p. 1131). After such a stimulus, however, the senses have a remarkable adaptability which allows them to rapidly return to a state of availability (p. 1153).

Valéry suggests that a sensation doesn't result from the introduction of something from the outside, but from an internal modification of an energetic system. It is as though a wire conducting electricity were momentarily touched by another wire, causing a brief disequilibrium, which then is the sensation (p. 1157). Elsewhere, he makes a separation between an external stimulus and an action of the mind itself, which looks in a new way on something familiar. The sensibility is something then which can be directed by the will, but the will has no direct action on sensations received (p. 1201), and the mind is limited by the action, limits and range of the senses of whose functioning we are unaware as we receive various sensations. We do not, however, 'see' the images on the retina, because the mind acts immediately upon them (p. 1162). Perception occurs because a sensation is significant and can be related to something already known (p. 1167). Thus perception in a way is antagonistic to sensation, and its operation can be disturbed by a superabundance of sense data. Thinking implies then a drastic reduction of sensations (p. 1192). Out of disorder, the mind creates order, but it must constantly return to the stimulus of disorder, and this disorder is re-created by our sensibility (p. 1180). There is, however, not always a simple movement from disorder to order. If the 'sensibilité générale' enters the functioning, an insignificant stimulus can create intellectual chaos. Again and again Valéry returns to the strange disproportion between causes and effects in the sensibility. He tries to distinguish the 'sensibilité générale', which is interior, subjective and even visceral, from the 'sensibilité spécialisée' which is linked to the senses and exterior stimuli (p. 1177). The power of the 'sensibilité générale' is so great that sometimes the capacity to respond will create the lacking demand. As in 'L'Abeille' of *Charmes* and *La Jeune Parque* ll. 174–8, boredom can produce activities which will divert it (p. 1195).

Mémoire

In this section, Valéry returns most frequently to the idea that memories serve the mind most by detaching themselves from their sources in order to become applicable to present situations. The most obvious example of this phenomenon is language (pp. 1217, 1240). These 'freed' memories, however, are not merely scattered in the brain. The memory maintains relationships between things (p. 1215), and this chain can be re-activitated by any one element. Practically every sensation will activate some memory, and it is only the completely 'new' sensation which would not be recognized: 'ce qui serait infiniment neuf échapperait à la connaissance — laquelle consiste à re-connaître' (p. 1237, variant b). Usually, when the mind receives sensations, the imagination goes to work and calls up various memories and combines them in a new construction (p. 1212). Valéry continually repeats the idea that it is memory which makes thought possible. 'La chose fondamentale est certainement la mémoire. Elle est comme la matière dont les modifications et les mouvements sont pensée' (p. 1229).

Statements like the preceding, however, do not give a full appreciation of the rapid and highly selective reductive and simplifying action of the memory (p. 1249). The memory always tends to economize mental work, something particularly obvious in the rapid re-orientation which occurs when a person wakes up. The self waking up recognizes itself as the 'same', although as Valéry points out, there is no sameness. However, 'sans ce souvenir inexact, pas de moi. — Toutes les fois qu'il y a souvenir, il y a illusion de conservation d'un soi' (pl 1230).

Temps

Throughout this section Valéry attempts many definitions of the 'present', beginning in 1901 with 'la seule chose continue' (p. 1263), and extending to 1944 with 'un *retour* à un *point* qui est le Moi' after any mental excursion (p. 1369). In 1914, however, the present was defined as interaction of the *moi* and the real world (p. 1273) and in 1930 as a form giving unity to the heterogeneity of real phenomena. This last formula appealed to Valéry because it permitted him to do away with the vague and usual idea of time and to replace it with time defined as an aspect of mental functioning (p. 1347). Valéry rejected the naive question 'What is time?', and even wanted to eliminate the word from the vocabulary. He criticized Bergson for his idea of *durée*. For Valéry there were many different *durées* defined by some specific concrete situation. Very early he made a division between times of which the mind is aware and others, such as times linked with vital functions. It was the first category which interested him. The commonest example of this time is noting that something we have seen before is now the same, but also different. Valéry notes that time seems to pass more quickly as we grow older because we rapidly recognize more things as things already seen.

The 'écart' creating a sense of time can be created in more subtle ways: a man watching a moving object only becomes aware of time when his eyes turn to something else (p. 1348). There is another time for a moment of crisis, and there can be occasions of crisis with two times. For a man running to catch a train time seems short, but at the same moment his fatigue makes time seem long. The mind going from incoherent inattention to thought and reflection introduces a new time (p. 1322). Reflection itself can have various times. Time linked with profound thought divorced from awareness of the surroundings is not the same as the time of thought interrupted by isolated sensations. Every mental specialization will have its own time (p. 1347).

Two types of mental specialization which particularly interested Valéry are rhythm and surprise. Rhythm was linked to Valéry's interest in poetry and other arts, but also with a general psychological interest: 'Tout réflexe dont la partie *réponse* est non instantanée et simple (c'est-à-dire d'une seule fonction) – est un élément rythmique' (p. 1276). He defined rhythm as a single unified emission, given in a certain order, indivisible, and always imitable. Its importance as a poetic effect can be seen in Valéry's insistence on the necessary relation between reactions of the senses to rhythm and effects on the muscles (p. 1340). The effects, however, are not just muscular, but imply a profound change of state, a 'specialization' of the mind with its own time (p. 1299). The particular time of crisis has already been mentioned. Surprise was one form of crisis which interested Valéry because of its novelty, and destruction of habits and pre-judgements. He frequently discusses 'attente', the mind constructed to face an anticipated future. Suddenly surprise through strangeness or intensity overwhelms expectations and creates 'oscillations': 'Il y a oscillation entre deux *temps* présents et une tentative de raccordement se dessine' (p. 1315). We cannot absorb the surprise because it arrives in the mind *before* memory and thus cannot be classified. This is the enormous value of surprise which disrupts the entire system of expectations (p. 1292).

CAHIERS (VOLUME II)

Rêve

Valéry wonders why the dreaming mind, far less complex than the conscious intellect, makes *changes* in familiar images (p. 191). There is an apparent explanation in the 'fête des fous' which is a reaction against the forces of reason dominating the waking state (pp. 50, 96). Valéry, however, is unwilling to give value to these mental activities. If a new idea seems to emerge from sleep, it is more likely a product of a refreshed sensibility (p. 145). He also refused value to the Freudian interpretations of dreams, and suggested that dreams were composed by instants and not continuities, whereas the awakened man inevitably sees dreams in terms of the alert mind and so creates continuities and adds to the dream a character it never had.

Thus, in contrast with André Breton and the Surrealists, Valéry's analysis is not Freudian but 'formal', attempting to define the elements and composition of the function in order to arrive at a better comprehension of the *conscious* mind (p. 106). First of all, the dreaming mind can't distinguish between 'demands' and 'responses' or between the three domains of world, body and mind (p. 180). The dreaming mind has no access to the immense context serving the awakened intellect. 'Ces objets, ces meubles, ces à-côtés qui semblent négligeables jouent le rôle capital d'empêcher une fraîcheur qui vient de la fenêtre ouverte de me convaincre que je suis au pôle au milieu des glaces' (pp. 121–2). The conscious mind *chooses* the mental images it needs and rejects the rest. This evaluating and neglecting function is absent in dreams and thus phenomena are dominant and not attention. The self and mental images are two ends of the same stick (pp. 39, 172). The immediate response to needs is the rule, and so chance, not choice, rules the sequence of images (p. 192). This frantic accumulation of chance images is stimulated by the radical incapacity of the dreaming mind to conserve and develop anything (p. 192). Thus in dreams there is no such thing as the act of reading, or *any* act (p. 194). There can then be no construction, and construction for Valéry is the great project and achievement of the conscious intellect (p. 68).

Conscience

The consciousness constantly detaches itself from anything, in order to turn to something else (pp. 211, 242), or simply in order to think about it (p. 219). To compensate for this separation, it must multiply its perspectives on reality (p. 220). Such thinking is highly aware of itself (p. 224), but perfect self-awareness is rare, in part because unconscious accompanies conscious functioning (pp. 232, 233). Conscious thought can become unconscious and automatic, and the opposite movement can occur (p. 208). It is conscious thinking which obtains Valéry's esteem and attention. It can begin by discovering new alternatives (p. 228). It can distinguish between various mental activities, between what is observed and what is presumed (p. 221). It reduces accumulated perspectives through the organization of ideas: disorder becomes order (p. 238). This organization can produce a new judgement different from the judgement of the separate parts (p. 228). The function of the unconscious interests Valéry much less. Still, as in 'Palme' of *Charmes*, he recognizes this hidden functioning (p. 226). Consciousness, however, must finally be the judge, and those who glorify the unconscious neglect the many times it fails to satisfy evaluation by conscious thought. He mocks the modern veneration of the unconscious (pp. 221, 231).

Attention

Attention is totally opposed to our habitual mental incoherence (p. 268). Valéry distinguishes between consciousness, which implies an awareness of the mental process, and attention, defined as an intense examination of ideas or things. One can be attentive without being self-aware. Valéry sees attention as an adjustment to a situation, analogous to an eye focussing on an object (p. 273). Attention implies a reduction of variables (p. 267), and a conservation and transformation of factors (p. 259). It is limited by fatigue (p. 268). Valéry tried to classify various forms of attention. In 1902 he established three categories: 1. waiting and watchful; 2. continuous and creative; 3. keeping one thing in mind while the rest of the mind varies (p. 254). In 1914 he considered another set of categories: '2 sortes d'attentions — bien distinctes. L'une *multiplie* les tâtonnements, l'autre essaie de les abolir — les *contient*' (p. 264).

Le Moi et la Personnalité

Valéry has a special definition of the 'Moi', which for him is an impersonal intellect, 'une simple condition de pensée' (p. 277), 'la sensation propre de l'activité cérébrale' (p. 280). A famous definition equates it with the mathematical zero (p. 296). It constantly frees itself and is forever new. A man is defined not by what he has done but by his possibilities. Conservation, however, is one of the functions of the 'Moi', although functional memory acts only as a pool of elements and doesn't dominate the mind (p. 320). The 'Moi' tries to reach maximum force and purity. One note anticipates the final pages of 'Note et Digression' of 1919 (O.I, pp. 1199–233): 'le grand égoïsme' contains other minds and is so luminous that it isn't represented by a man or a name (p. 284). Opposed to this 'Moi' is the personality which defines and limits. It is accidental, a result of memories, habits, phobias. Men like to think it is constant, but Valéry affirms that it is shifting and at best periodic.

Affectivité

Most of this section discusses the destructive role of emotions in intellectual life, although a few notes consider their positive functions. Some notes marvel over the disproportion between the causes and effects of emotions (pp. 347, 349), while others consider emotions as a malfunctioning of the mind which can't dissipate certain energies (p. 364). Valéry is sceptical of the importance accorded spontaneous emotions (p. 339). He comments also on ingrained likes and dislikes never scrutinized by the critical mind (pp. 372, 387). Sometimes the mind abdicates totally and yields completely to feelings, and Valéry gives an interesting analysis of tears and laughter and other convulsive reactions which replace 'idées nettes' (p. 350). This abdication, however, can be fruitful if the mind reacts by a counter-attack (p. 357). As Valéry says in the section entitled 'Poésie':

La Poésie est l'essai de représenter par les moyens du langage articulé, ces *cooses* ou cette *chose*, que tentent obscurément d'exprimer les cris, les larmes, silences, les caresses, les baisers, les soupirs etc. (pp. 1099–100)

Eros

Between 1892 and 1920, Valéry's ideas on love were primarily influenced by a ridiculous passion he had had for a married woman, Madame de Rovira, seen only on several occasions, and with whom Valéry never spoke. Thus love is seen as a dubious cultural phenomenon, a literary fabrication created by authors in search of a subject, a set of clichés (p. 404). Love depends on *not* knowing the other, and its 'union' is really a mutilation, excluding all that won't feed the folly of the couple. It is an embellishment added to the essential sex act. As for the sex act itself, it astonishes Valéry: 'Qui déchiffrera l'énigme de cette folie? Une telle furie n'était pas nécessaire à la propagation d'une espèce' (p. 404). It is a levelling force of repetitive acts, a disgusting performance, although less disgusting than sentimentality (p. 401). A few notes in this period, however, find utility in love and sex. It is an augmentation of energy which can be used in some productive manner, or else it is a means toward greater knowledge of self (p. 401).

The liaison with Catherine Pozzi enriches the positive view even if this affair was short and caused suffering almost from the start. The gifted Catherine Pozzi became Valéry's mistress in September 1920. Apparently Valéry's love was the greater of the two (p. 416), and apparently Valéry was forced to choose between family and mistress (p. 459), causing an abrupt end on 23 October 1921. But until 1928 when he met Renée Vautier, Valéry suffered, and as late as 1930 he had distressing memories. In September 1931 he seems in love with the sculptress Renée Vautier, but this affair also turned out badly, as did a third liaison in 1941 when Valéry was 70. These unhappy liaisons impressed Valéry with the terrible power of love. An early 'resonance' soon becomes irrationality (p. 528), and when things go badly, recurring torments paralyse the mind. The very difference of two people produces power struggles and inevitable separation. Valéry wanted his power for himself, refused to be dominated, and said that only in the self can one find the key to one's existence. So he can sum up his liaison with Catherine Pozzi with 'Histoire d'un Voyage: de l'Orgueil à l'Amour (et retour—)' (p. 433). His idea of poetry also rejected love as a theme (p. 535).

Concurrently with these negations, however, Valéry expressed very different views. The extreme form of existence demands the total reckless gift of the self, and only one thing counts: the exchange of what is most precious in a man and a woman (p. 449). Mere sex attraction doesn't explain the need two lovers have for one another, and in his union with Catherine, he found 'une intelligence parfaite entre des systèmes vivants' (p. 455) where they could 'perdre ensemble le plus qu'ils pussent de leur différence' (p. 456). Such unions can be models for the relation of the self with the self (p. 456).

The mind played an important role in Valéry's relations with Catherine. He could love deeply only an intelligent woman, and he found that sexual activity stimulated the intellect (p. 535). An important note offers a synthesis of physical love, intellectual exchange and even the physical surroundings in a union of lovers (p. 485). A later note from 1941 gives a more precise explanation of this synthesis and union. Here it is clear that the union is never complete because the 'Moi' doesn't lose its identity. That doesn't prevent the union from being intensely felt (pp. 540–1).

Thêta

There are hardly any notes approving religion in this section. In 1899 Valéry finds that religion offers possibilities for studying the mind (pp. 565–6), and in 1921 he speaks approvingly of prayer (p. 605). Valéry's own religion is the pursuit of the highest intellectual values and his Saints are great thinkers of the past (p. 566). His morality is not causing pain to others, and his attitude toward death is also succinct: 'La mort n'a pas plus de rapport avec la vie (consciente) que la rupture d'un vase avec sa figure' (p. 595). His irreligion comes from the small value he places on himself and others (p. 603), and also from his *pudeur* (p. 593) and refusal to adopt something he wouldn't have invented (p. 568), and also from his idea of purity: 'S'il y avait un Dieu, il n'y aurait que lui, pas de monde' (p. 602), which recalls ll. 28–30 of 'Ebauche d'un Serpent' in *Charmes*. But primarily Valéry's objections are intellectual ones. Religion limits use of the brain (p. 570), whereas 'je ne suis que Recherche' (p. 624). Religion is a *mélange impur* resting on miracles and requiring faith in the unknowable (p. 662). The language of religion doesn't lead to recognizable things (p. 698). The questions it poses are naive and without sense (pp. 645, 697), and the answers to those questions are created by the self (p. 684). The explanation of religion is in human fears, self-interest, feelings of impotence and injustice (p. 660). Thus religion is anti-humanist, opposed to invention, construction, incredulity, a bold mind, *orgueil* (p. 596). Christ, without an intellectual and sexual life, is a questionable example of humanity, and the Devil offers Him only mediocre temptations (p. 704).

Bios

Valéry's methods are interesting in this section. He tries to arrive at definitions by the use of great contrasts (man/nature), basic relationships (living beings and environment), or essential factors (of life). The contrast man/nature keeps him from anthropomorphic tendencies, while his scepticism regarding unproved theories causes him to express doubts about evolution (p. 763). Valéry defines 'life' by its internal acts of transformation and conservation and also by its cycles, which contrast it with the mind (p. 749). Also, the inorganic body is not isolated from its milieu and is constantly being broken down, while the living body adapts itself to its milieu and modifies it, and is characterized by its organizing and constructive aspects (p. 745). He contrasts man and animals. If human intelligence is non-repetitive, animal behaviour is cyclical and without real freedom (pp. 757–8). Speculations on the contrast man/nature are more frequent. Their methods of construction are opposed (p. 752). Thus the origins and nature of life are incomprehensible for man. Man's action is the result of a series of challenges from his milieu (pp. 733–4). He believes himself unique and essential and tries to preserve himself, but this instinct is really a part of the grand action of nature which finally absorbs him (p. 755).

Mathématiques

In 1896, Valéry writes in his *Cahiers*: 'S'amuser à tenter de traduire tout en mathématiques' (p. 777). Mathematics appears in this section as an ideal model of the mind's functioning. First, it is an activity which permits maximum self-awareness (p. 779). Secondly, mathematics is a model of totally controlled thinking, using a rigorous language (p. 801). But it is no mere mechanical process. Rather, it is a model of mental audacity and invention (pp. 804, 815). Valéry sees mathematics as a transformation exploiting formal properties (p. 824). Liberty and audacity permit then a complete development, or 'exhaustion' of the problem (pp. 803, 787).

Science

Valéry was well-acquainted with modern physics and mathematics through reading and personal contacts, and he believed firmly in the importance of questions raised by the informed non-specialist (pp. 867, 896). Most notes here show Valéry's familiarity with the procedures and achievements of modern science. It depends on the means man has for operating on physical reality. It advances not by vast general theories but by the 'mot à mot' (848), and it uses precise language and rigorous verifiable procedures (p. 903). Modern science is moving toward increasing complexity and loss of 'continuity' rather than logical convergence (pp. 901, 904). It uses 'relays' to make indirect contact with phenomena too small to be seen directly (p. 887). Its progress is marked by an increase of problems and questions (p. 870), by an increased awareness and increased organization and connections (p. 836), and finally by power over the material world through action and prediction (pp. 861, 907).

Art et Esthétique

This section emphasizes the importance of the formal approach in the creative process (p. 927), and of 'modulations', smooth transitions, between parts of a work of art (pp. 937, 956, 958). It stresses the exigencies, rigour, and long hard work of the true artist and criticizes modern artists who yield to facility and employ surprise and shock-effects (p. 983). The studied techniques of the ideal artist must, however, remain finally invisible (p. 941). With economy of means he must obtain an abundance of effects (p. 924), a multiplicity of meanings (p. 942). The beauty of this complex object can never be exhausted, and it remains finally inexplicable (pp. 953, 954, 944). Art is not destined to 'serve humanity' but to create an exalted state (p. 940). Various forms of this beauty succeed each other historically in a pattern of rotation (p. 953). But when it comes to modern painting, Valéry refuses to accept the forms he finds, and comments on the facility of modern painters, their lack of skill, and failure to exploit developments.

Monet, however, is not included in this condemnation, and
Valéry several times admires the poetry and singing quality of
his colours (pp. 948, 949).

Valéry admired Egyptian sculpture for its rigour and the world
of dreams it evokes (p. 961), and Greek architecture for its clear
separation of parts and functions, analogous to geometry (p. 941).
Gothic architecture is praised for its unity and modulations which
reminded Valéry of the world of plants (pp. 981, 937). He was,
however, highly critical of modern architecture (p. 958). His
admiration for Wagner's music was immense (pp. 956, 980, 979).
It simulates movements of the mind and acts powerfully on the
nervous system (p. 930). At times Valéry the poet envies the
composer (p. 951), but at other times he fears the powerful effects
of music on the emotions (pp. 936, 938). Valéry also admired
Gluck (pp. 938, 960), Mozart, and he felt intensely the purity of
the music of Bach (p. 955). Perhaps his admiration for both
Wagner and Bach is expressed in a comment on the dual nature
of music, both 'visceral' and 'structural' (p. 973). For him 'La
grandiose Musique est l'écriture de l'homme complet' (p. 930).

Littérature

Valéry is against modern literature, critics and readers. Modern
literature is not something he would wish to commit to memory,
nor does it increase our intellectual powers (p. 1225). Modern
writers yield to facility and the temptation of doing something new
rather than something better. Valéry criticizes the enlargement of
vocabulary, and accuses the temptation of the *pittoresque* of
destroying syntax (p. 1217). Good readers are corrupted by the
facile prose of newspapers and magazines. Valéry wants elite
readers and is sceptical of any art with wide appeal (p. 1167).
Literary critics reveal only their preferences and try to reconstruct
the person of the author. Instead they should attempt to discover
what the author was trying to do in his writing (p. 1191). Other
comments attack the modern taste for confessions (p. 1160) and
the genre of the novel. Valéry anticipated somewhat the theories
of present-day French 'New Novelists'. He is little interested by
characters and *récits* (p. 1187); he separates novels from reality
(p. 1158); and he places *art* above everything (p. 1222). Despite
his aversion for novels, he is charmed by Stendhal (p. 1220) and

especially by Restif de la Bretonne, where he finds 'toute une France disparue' (pp. 1230, 1231).

Valéry classifies Shakespeare among the 'moderns' (p. 1185). He attacks Molière for destroying 'le théâtre profond' (p. 1193). Not even Racine escapes criticism (p. 1229). Racine, however, re-discovered by Valéry when he was writing *La Jeune Parque*, is generally praised, and it is Racine who corresponds to Valéry's sensibility and not Shakespeare (p. 1184). Valéry also expresses admiration for the late nineteenth-century Symbolists (p. 1180), and he attempts to define Symbolist poetry (p. 1176).

Sujets

Here there are many projects of plays, poems, short stories, novellas, dialogues, monologues, even a ballet. One passage (pp. 1318–20) anticipates a section of 'Eupalinos' (O.II, pp. 116–30); another offers a possible conclusion for 'Fragments du Narcisse' in *Charmes* (p. 1327); many others have ideas for *Mon Faust* (O.II, pp. 276–403); still others contain ideas for the Teste cycle (O.II, pp. 11–75). There are many notes for a drama on Tiberius, viewed as a realistic, logical, self-dominating intellect, and for a tragedy on Stratonice, which would have treated the theme of the mind trapped in unhappy love. We see Valéry's predilection for the dialogue, so adapted to the conscious mind's activity (pp. 1314, 1315). One of these projects (p. 1313) anticipates a part of *L'Idée Fixe* (O.II, p. 249), where a story is told about a duel of magicians, one attempting to devour the other. Both passages recall a note on 'le grand égoïsme' in the *Cahier* section 'Le Moi et la Personnalité' (p. 284). A project for a 'Psalm' further elaborates the desire for universality by imagining an angel imprisoned in the body of a man (p. 1325). A project for a novella presents a man moving toward universality by rejecting daily trivialities (p. 1335). A more strikingly original similar project for a short story imagines another man drawing lots for all the decisions of his existence (p. 1321).

Homo

Valéry measures men not by their acts but by their intentions (p. 1363). These are best defined by their abstentions, and these abstentions are hard to discover (p. 1373). As for *political* action, a keen awareness of intellectual limits and of the complexity of reality caused Valéry to be sceptical: 'Que de choses il faut ignorer pour "agir" ' (p. 1380). Furthermore, Valéry's method of adopting *various* perspectives (see the section on 'Philosophie') resulted in a rejection of partisan attitudes (pp. 1418, 1422). Finally, politics seemed to him an impure and trivial activity concerned with superficial events (p. 1436). Valéry's intellectual heroism was directed toward a more elevated level than political activity. His ambition was complete self-reconstruction (p. 1386), maximum self-awareness as contrasted with mere erudition (p. 1386), universal domination (p. 1360), and rivalry with the gods (p. 1387). Rather than being motivated by love for humanity, he is driven by a need to rise above humanity (p. 1362). Such a programme demands great self-discipline (p. 1367), a rejection of the tranquil immobility of *bonheur* (p. 1404), and an obedience to an ideal, which Valéry calls *orgueil* (p. 1392). This *orgueil* creates intellectual solitude and independence (pp. 1416, 1417). One should not exaggerate Valéry's isolation, however. In *Cahiers*, section 'Science', he gives great importance to personal contacts and conversations with experts, and in 'Homo' he states firmly: 'On n'arrive au sommet de soi-même que par le détour et le secours des autres' (p. 1409). Nor should we exaggerate Valéry's 'heroism', which was certainly his ideal, but not always his reality. Repeatedly he emphasizes the superficiality and uselessness of most of our ideas, and the limits of intelligence (pp. 1362, 1406, 1408, 1416). Other notes reveal his awareness of the dark side of the mind, with its absurdities, stupidities, and abominations (p. 1379). This intellectual hero concedes that there is value in our ingrained habits and customs (p. 1382). Another note affirms the need to join Dionysus with Apollo and not separate one from the other (p. 1381). Finally, in a remark which recalls 'Le Cimetière Marin', Valéry emphasizes the necessary acceptance of 'life', such as it is, without illusions (p. 1440).

This section also contains a critique of human moralities and human justice. Man is naturally egocentric, without natural moral impulses (pp. 1389, 1400, 1406), and moralities in order to work need some suspect motive (p. 1361). Thus it is much better for the mind to free itself from so-called moral impulses (p. 1367). A man should do good through awareness, not morality, and thus should be equally capable of doing evil (p. 1371). The mind may even be more effective than morality for resisting temptations (p. 1381). Moralities are not only opposed to the intellect, but to what makes man an individual (p. 1379). They fail to take account of the infinite complexity of man (p. 1391). The very bases of the moralist's reasoning lack rigour and profundity (p. 1364).

The reasoning of criminal justice is equally superficial, particularly in the theory of responsibility. Valéry points out that man's consciousness does not control the causes of a criminal act, nor is it capable of foreseeing the consequences (pp. 1391, 1395). Furthermore, society punishes only the crimes of which it is aware; the others go unpunished (p. 1410). Punishment is a negotiation, a bargaining, with crime (p. 1396). And if a court of justice is a market-place, it is also a theatre — with neat dénouements (p. 1422).

Histoire et Politique

Valéry was highly critical of historians, for their methodology, pretensions, and the evil role they played in world politics, perpetuating old hatreds. He accused them of ignoring significant events like the discovery of electricity, of trusting too much to one perspective, of talking loosely of 'causes' and 'facts', and of excessively rationalizing what is really a chaos (pp. 1495, 1496). Working on accounts of events they haven't witnessed, they make prophecies for the future based on 'lessons' of the past. Even Napoleon is guilty of these practices (pp. 1490, 1526, 1542). More often, however, Valéry admired Napoleon and praised him for his vision of the reality of his own time (p. 1449). Other notes stress his ability for organization, his methodology and reasoning powers, his imagination and capacity for execution (p. 1449).

When Valéry was making his first admiring comments on Napoleon, he was also writing his first notes critical of democracy, to which he always preferred a hierarchical government run by an elite (pp. 1448, 1461). In a democracy people are manipulated by theatrical effects and are incapable of studying problems. All is directed toward immediate satisfactions, and the carrying out of great conceptions becomes impossible (p. 1454). Valéry finds, however, that France has fared no better under dictatorships (p. 1513), and so he is sceptical of all politics. He is opposed to political parties because they limit thought (p. 1482), and he is scandalized by power-hungry leaders (p. 1491). Leaders are generally ignorant, a minority holding power for the benefit of a minority. Valéry sees the majority tyrannized by the powerful modern state (pp. 1506, 1537). Everywhere men's lives are invaded, and their tastes and opinions manipulated by publicity, press and cinema. Everywhere particularity gives way to conformity (pp. 1502, 1516). At the same time Valéry favoured internationalism and a united Europe, and he deplored the recourse to war. In 1936, visiting Munich, he commented on the brutal and childish air of the S.S. troops (p. 1495). When defeat came in 1940, however, despite all his harsh criticisms of democracy, politics, the French, and the modern world, Valéry chose not to seek out the guilty parties, but looked instead to the future (p. 1503). Unlike the historians he attacked, he refused to be a prisoner of the past (p. 1507).

Enseignement
Valéry, with bad memories of his own early education (p. 1580), accuses the schools of killing the natural curiosity of children. He emphasizes the importance of creating a *need* in the child for instruction. The teacher should communicate the basic ideas of mathematics rather than procedures (p. 1559). Schooling must move outside the classroom to teach the child to observe the natural world in which he lives (p. 1559). and it must prepare the child for living in society. Above all, school should teach the child to think originally, to puzzle over his own problems rather than those given him by others. The teacher must cultivate the child's essential intellectual functions (p. 1574). Those who would reduce Valéry to a narrow rationalist should consider the importance he gives here to the cultivation of the imagination and sensibility (pp. 1555, 1573). Several notes criticize sharply the inept teaching of poetry (pp. 1560, 1577, 1579). If poetry is badly taught, it is in large part because all instruction is oriented toward examinations where poems and profound ideas are debased into test questions (p. 1557). Those who are successful in these examinations are rewarded with privileged careers where they may stagnate until retirement (p. 1570).

LITERARY FORTUNES AND INFLUENCE

The first full recognition of Valéry's importance as a twentieth-century poet came not in France but in England where *La Jeune Parque* was reviewed at length by John Middleton Murry in the *T.L.S.* of 23 August 1917. Then on 11 April and 2 May 1919, Murry published in *The Athenaeum* 'The Spiritual Crisis' and 'The Intellectual Crisis', later to appear in France as 'La Crise de l'Esprit' (O.I, pp. 988–1000). These were followed in the 27 August 1920 number by J. W. N. Sullivan's long discussion of Valéry's 'Introduction à la Méthode de Léonard de Vinci'. In April 1923, T. S. Eliot published Mark Wardle's translation of Valéry's 'Ebauche d'un Serpent' in *The Criterion*, and the following year the poem appeared as a separate volume with an important introduction by Eliot.

Murry's *Jeune Parque* article increased serious interest in Britain in the French Symbolist movement. Through Valéry, English poets, for example Edith Sitwell and T. S. Eliot, were able to reach a better understanding of the possibilities of Symbolist poetry. There is no direct influence of Valéry's poetry on Eliot's, however, and Eliot's earliest comments on the French poet, contained in an essay on Dante, are rather critical of some of Valéry's ideas. Eliot emphasizes Valéry's opposition to 'philosophical poetry' and mentions Valéry's definition of the aim of poetry: 'de produire en nous un *état* et de porter cet état exceptionnel au point d'une jouissance parfaite.' Eliot then remarks: 'A state, in itself, is nothing whatever.'[1] To Valéry's definition, Eliot opposes the example of Dante:

Dante, more than any other poet, has succeeded in dealing with his philosophy, not as a theory . . . but in terms of something *perceived*.
. . .
We are not here studying the philosophy, we *see* it, as part of the ordered world. The aim of the poet is to state a vision . . .[2]

In a much later article, Eliot was sceptical of Valéry's speculations about the absence of subject matter in *poésie pure*. 'I think that poetry is only poetry so long as it preserves some 'impurity' in this sense: that is to say, so long as the subject matter is valued for its own sake.'³ Finally, in an introduction to *The Art of Poetry* in the Bollingen Collected Works of Valéry, Eliot attacks one of the essential elements of Valéry's poetics: the utilization of a special poetic vocabulary, separate from the vocabulary of prose. Eliot suggests that if the idiom, vocabulary and syntax of poetry depart from prose, they will be remote from speech, and the language of poetry will become more and more artificial. 'In assimilating poetry to music, Valéry has, it seems to me, failed to insist upon its relation to speech.'⁴

These adverse comments, however, hardly occupy a major place in what Eliot has written about Valéry. In his 'Leçon de Valéry', Eliot says that his intimacy with Valéry's poetry was largely due to his study of what Valéry had written about poetry, and he emphasizes that again and again he found that Valéry's analyses of the poetic process corresponded to his own experience and illuminated aspects which had previously been obscure.⁵ In the same article he recounts that he met Valéry several times between 1924 and 1945, and he praises his 'impish' wit and 'unaffected modesty'. 'His modesty and his informality were the qualities of a man without illusions, who maintained no pretence about himself to himself, and found it idle to pretend to others.'⁶ His highest praise, however, is for Valéry as a great poet of the modern period. 'It is he who will remain for posterity the representative poet, the symbol of the poet, of the first half of the twentieth century — not Yeats, not Rilke, not anyone else.'⁷ Already in his introduction to *Le Serpent* in 1924, Eliot had affirmed that Valéry's greatness was in his reintegration of the experimental work of the Symbolist movement into the great tradition of classicism. Later, in 1949, Eliot saw Baudelaire, Mallarmé and Valéry as the beginning, the middle and the end of a certain form of poetry, and in 1952 he expanded this idea, seeing in Valéry the end of an entire era:

Finally, when Valéry died, in 1945, his death seemed to mark the end of an age, with greater definitiveness and solemnity than that of any other European author of his generation could have done. What Valéry represented, in his total *œuvre* — for his poetry and his critical and speculative prose form one inseparable whole — was the perfection, the culmination of a type of civilized mind which becomes, to the post-war world, increasingly alien.[8]

Eliot rightly emphasized the great influence of Poe on Valéry, suggesting that it was in Poe's writings that Valéry found the idea that a poem should have nothing in view but itself. It is through Poe that Valéry became a distinctly modern poet, modern because so completely self-conscious. 'Valéry in fact invented, and was to impose upon his age, not so much a new conception of poetry as a new conception of the poet. The tower of ivory has been fitted up as a laboratory. . .'[9] Eliot well understood, however, that this laboratory technician was a creator of beautiful forms appealing to those emotions stimulated by great art:

One is prepared for art when one has ceased to be interested in one's own emotions and experiences except as material; and when one has reached this point of indifference one will pick and choose according to very different principles from the principles of those people who are still excited by their own feelings and passionately enthusiastic over their own passions. And observe that, as M. Thibaudet well says, Valéry's interest in 'technique' is something much more comprehensive than an interest in the skilful disposition of words for their own sake: it is a recognition of the truth that not our feelings, but the pattern which we make of our feelings, is the centre of value.[10]

Already in 1924, Eliot was demolishing the tenacious cliché of Valéry the 'intellectual' poet:

It is a further error to conceive of Valéry as an 'intellectual' poet, in contrast to poets of emotion and vivid depiction of life. Poetry, the product, is neither more nor less intellectual; but it is written by men some of whom are more intellectual and some less — they may write equally good poetry.[11]

At the same time that T. S. Eliot was showing an interest in Valéry in England, Rilke in Germany was strongly attracted by Valéry's poetry, although for rather different reasons. In 1922 Rilke wrote: 'Paul Valéry continue à m'occuper par-dessus tout.'[12] He translated almost all of *Charmes* as well as 'L'Ame et la Danse' and 'Eupalinos'. As Judith Ryan has shown in a perceptive article, however, it is questionable how much Rilke actually 'learned' from Valéry.[13] The translations were almost all made after Rilke had completed *Duineser Elegien* and *Die Sonette an*

Orpheus, and if Rilke felt a strong affinity for Valéry's poetry and ideas, it was largely because he saw the French poet through his own attitudes. In detailed analysis, Professor Ryan has shown how Rilke in his translation of 'Le Cimetière Marin' imposed his own favourite ideas on the poem. Rilke's understanding of the functioning of the creative imagination was really quite different from Valéry's. Instead of drawing images from the real world for the sake of comparison, Valéry habitually *begins* with a mental image, something already internalized like the 'moutons mystérieux' (l. 63) or the 'toit tranquille' (l. 1) of 'Le Cimetière Marin', and then he develops the image through further mental reflection.

In Italy, Valery knew the poet Giuseppe Ungaretti, and both poets were united in an admiration for Mallarmé. Like Eliot, Ungaretti was interested in what Valéry wrote about poetic creation and was impressed by the idea of the *homo faber*, but as in the case of Eliot there is no visible resemblance between Ungaretti's poetry and that of Paul Valéry. In Spain, the writer Eugenio d'Ors was a friend of Valéry, but this admirer of the classical tradition seems far closer to Charles Maurras. More important is the affinity between Valéry and Juan Ramon Jiménez, drawn, after 1917, toward a *poésie pure* placed under the sign of the intelligence. Yet Jorge Guillén, discussing the poets of the generation of 1898 who were writing between 1920 and 1936, and noting that the foreign poets most read and loved in Spain were the French, from Baudelaire to the Surrealists, cautions against any significant influence exerted by Valéry:

Poésie pure then, 'pure poetry'? This platonic idea could never take form in a concrete body. None among us dreamed of such absolute purity, none desired it, not even the author of *Cantico*, a book which can be defined negatively as the antithesis of Valéry's *Charmes*. Valéry, read and reread with great devotion by the Castilian poet, was a model of exemplary elevation of subject matter and of exemplary rigor of style — with the light of a poetic consciousness. In the tradition of Edgar Allan Poe, Valéry believed scarcely or not at all in 'inspiration' — on which these Spanish poets were always dependent. . .[14]

Nor is the great Argentinian writer Jorge Borges to be considered any more directly influenced by Valéry than these Peninsular poets. Gérard Genette, however, has shown that Borges and Valéry have the same ideas about the creation of forms in art: the true creator is not the avant-garde artist who invents something radically new; he is instead the artist capable of exploiting an old form which has become again appropriate.[15] More recently, Professor Loubère has shown an interesting resemblance between Borges' manner of looking at the world, his attitudes toward the mysteries of reality, and Valéry's.[16] There are many witty allusions to Valéry in Borges' story, 'Pierre Ménard, autor del *Quijote*' in *Ficciones*, and Loubère shows similarities between a number of other fantastic stories by Borges and Valéry's own tales and outlines for stories in the *Cahiers*. Both writers are seeking far more than the astonishing anecdote. Both are using the fantastic as a way of dealing with the ambushes concealed in the burgeoning universe. Both are unwilling to be caught out by the unexpected.[17]

In France, in 1914, the eighteen-year old André Breton dedicated a sonnet entitled 'Rieuse' to Paul Valéry, and the two poets corresponded with each other. Breton later claimed that he knew 'La Soirée avec Monsieur Teste' almost by heart and in 1952 he called it Valéry's finest creation.[18] He admired particularly Valéry's 'Silence' and rejection of a conventional literary career, and so the publication of *La Jeune Parque* in 1917 appeared to Breton as a betrayal, and greatly damaged his friendship with Valéry. Still, in a poll conducted by *Littérature* in 1921, Breton gave a 15 out of a possible 20 (certainly an honourable score on the French grading scale) to Paul Valéry, and in March 1919 *Littérature* (the Surrealist review) published Valéry's 'Le Cantique des Colonnes' and in February 1920 his 'Ode Secrète'. H. S. Gershman has indicated similarities between Valéry's ideas on the origin of poetic inspiration with Breton's,[19] but as E. Gaède has pointed out in a criticism of Gershman's article, he neglects to mention *Notes sur la Poésie*, published by Breton and Eluard in 1936, a little volume which wittily mocks Valéry's ideas on poetry by turning them upside-down:[20]

A la moindre rature, le principe d'inspiration totale est ruiné. L'im-bécillité efface ce que l'oreille a prudemment *créé*.

. . .

L'existence de la poésie est essentiellement certaine; de quoi l'on doit s'enorgueillir. Sur ce point, elle ressemble au Diable.

. . .

Un poème doit être une débâcle de l'intellect. Il ne peut être autre chose. Débâcle: c'est un sauve-qui-peut, mais solennel, mais probant; image de ce qu'on devrait être, de l'état où les efforts ne comptent plus.

Like Breton, Jean-Paul Sartre appears to have read Valéry well, borrowing certain expressions and ideas such as the separation of poetry and prose, an idea Sartre exploited in 'Qu'est-ce que la littérature?' But as with Breton there is no profound relationship between the two men, and any apparent similarities reveal upon examination significant divergences, as Laurent Le Sage has demonstrated. Professor Le Sage mentions Valéry's ideas on language:

Particularly in his diaries Valéry ponders the problem of language as mediator of the world. Vocabulary and syntax dictate to men all that the world can mean. Valéry seems closer here to the structuralists than to Sartre; actually he is probably closer to men of his own generation who asserted repeatedly the importance of language.[21]

Contemporary Structuralists have, in fact, paid a great deal of attention to Valéry's ideas. Tzvetan Todorov, however, has concluded that Valéry is not a Structuralist in his poetics, because he is primarily interested in exploring the creative process, as T. S. Eliot had noted, whereas the Structuralists are attempting to create a 'literary discourse' including all literary means, or uses of language. Still, Todorov emphasizes that Valéry has a close affinity with modern criticism. He *sees* literature like the Structuralists, and it is only his approach which is different. Todorov repeats Gérard Genette's suggestion that Valéry resembles formalist critics.[22] Genette had said that Valéry is close not only to the Russian formalists of the 1920s, but also to the American New Critics. He finds a Structuralist attitude, however, in Valéry's way of thinking and quotes this well-known passage (where the influence of Henri Poincaré is clearly discernible): 'Il y eut un temps où je voyais. Je voyais ou voulais voir les figures de relations entre les choses, et non les choses. Les choses me faisaient sourire de pitié. Ceux qui s'y arrêtaient ne m'étaient que des idolâtres. Je savais que l'essentiel était figure.'[23]

It is Jacques Derrida who explores the Structuralist attitude in a much-quoted article.[24] He examines Valéry's ideas on the 'source' within the creating person, pointing out that the *origin cannot be discovered,* and refers to the Hegelian notion that the origin is in the *result,* and this in turn recalls Lacan's affirmation that the origin, or person, is really revealed in the structure of the chain of speech. Derrida concludes by marking the opposition between Valéry and Freud in an interesting discussion of Valéry's theory of the 'implexe' (see p. 73 above, for Valery's explanation of this term). For Derrida, the 'implexe' is a complex of the present moment, *multiplying* the simplicity of the source, and making it impossible for the present moment ever to offer itself as a simple and punctual origin.

Nicole Celeyrette-Pietri, in an interesting article, pursues the very same theme as Derrida, but from the point of view of linguistics.[25] In Valéry's *Cahiers* there is no real linguistic theory, but there are many very provocative fragments. Valéry shows himself aware of the great importance of pronouns, to which modern linguists like E. Benveniste and R. Jakobson have called attention. Studying the pronoun *je,* Valéry begins with an idea confirmed by present-day linguistic study: *je* is not a part of primitive language but a recent phenomenon. Valéry admires this creation, but at the same time attacks it as the origin of a pernicious myth, the permanence of the unified person. He shows that usually *je* doesn't replace a name, but is merely an empty sign, and he tries to see what, in each example, can replace *je.* Even our everyday language shows the artificiality of the first person. Next to 'je me souviens' we have 'il me souvient', affirming the autonomy of memory. After exploring Valéry's various approaches to the pronoun, however, Madame Celeyrette-Pietri concludes her article with this important caution:

Mais les réflexions théoriques des *Cahiers,* si minutieuses, si riches d'intuitions, semblent parfois tourner court et manquent un peu de cohérence, faute en particulier d'une terminologie précise, que Valéry, on peut s'en étonner, ne s'est guère efforcé de mettre au point.[26]

Gérard Genette, in the article already mentioned above, not only noted links between Valéry and the formalists and structuralists, but also between Valéry and the French 'New Novelists'. Jean Ricardou in particular, a 'New Novelist' perhaps better-known as a theorist of the new novel, has often referred to Valéry in his essays. Ricardou approves Valéry's opposition to 'humanism', by which he means Valéry's refusal, in his poetry, to indulge in too 'human' emotions, themes, and situations. Above all, Ricardou approves Valéry's attack on the myth of 'expression', the myth of the author who 'has something to say', the myth of 'sincerity', and of course these themes form the very foundation of Ricardou's own theoretical writings. An accompanying myth is 'the author' who presumably contains within his person whatever the reader has managed to discover in his writings. On the positive side, Ricardou shares Valéry's respect for 'work' (as opposed to facile 'inspiration'), 'un travail du texte à partir d'*un dispositif formel* et de *la matière du langage* . . . Il suit que les idées, loin d'être inductrices du texte, ne sont que les conséquences d'une certaine pratique scripturale.'[27]

There are even more specific anticipations of the French New Novel. 'Valéry reproche surtout au roman . . . d'encourager l'illusion réaliste. . .'[28] Neither Valéry nor Ricardou believe in the 'existence' or 'psychology' of the characters of a novel. The old notion of 'verisimilitude' also comes under attack. Ricardou quotes a note from Valéry's *Cahiers*: 'J'ai songé à un roman qui irait délibérément "contre la vérité" — au sens des romanciers. Mais fait de personnages et de solutions *construits*', and Ricardou mentions as examples of such novels, *Le Voyeur* by Robbe-Grillet, *L'Emploi du Temps* by Butor, *La Mise en Scène* by Ollier, and *Le Parc* by Sollers. Like Genette, he quotes one of Valéry's speculations:

Peut-être serait-il intéressant de faire *une fois* une œuvre qui montrerait, à chacun de ses *nœuds*, la diversité qui peut s'y présenter à l'esprit et parmi laquelle il *choisit* la suite unique qui sera donnée dans le texte. Ce serait là substituer à l'illusion d'une détermination unique et imitatrice du réel, celle du *possible à chaque instant* qui me semble plus véritable.

As examples of such a novel, Ricardou mentions Robbe-Grillet's *La Jalousie* and Pinget's *Passacaille*, while Genette adds Soller's *Le Parc* and Robbe-Grillet's *Le Voyeur*.

T. S. Eliot said that Valéry as a civilized man and Valéry as a symbolist poet marked the end of an era, an era closed by the ending of the second world war. And yet so many of Valéry's ideas, written down in his *Cahiers* over a period of fifty years, are now alive in France more than thirty years after his death. Was

Valéry perhaps right in affirming that his most important work was in those notebooks? The irregular sonnet, 'Le Vin Perdu' in *Charmes* now seems prophetic. It is a poem about death, about wine poured into the ocean, wine which is at the same time an offering, the poet's life-blood, and his cherished ideas. In the first tercet, the wine seems to disappear without leaving any trace, but in the final stanza the ocean is transformed, and the poet sees a vision of 'figures profondes' leaping in the bitter air:

> Perdu ce vin, ivres les ondes! . . .
> J'ai vu bondir dans l'air amer
> Les figures les plus profondes . . .

VIII

VALERY AND THE CRITICS

Sans doute, parmi tous les écrivains à qui n'a pas été dévolue une véritable vocation scientifique, Valéry s'est avancé plus loin que quiconque sur la route: il ne s'est pas seulement approprié les méthodes,—tour de force bien autrement surprenant, il a su incorporer à sa pensée personnelle—qui par là semble toujours reliée à l'ensemble de l'univers—les résultats essentiels de la science. . . De son contact avec la science, Valéry retient l'idée des rapports,—la seule qui ne se désagrège pas instantanément sous son regard. Il la retient, et c'est en elle qu'il se découvre enfin la porte d'évasion. Maître dans l'art de 'la jonction délicate, mais naturelle, de dons distincts', il opère un transfert, et c'est le transfert dans le domaine des mots de l'idée scientifique des rapports. Les rapports de mots, voilà l'*ultima Thule* à laquelle se tient, que peut encore priser l'homme universellement dépris. . .

Charles Du Bos, *Approximations*, Fayard, 1965, p. 45.

Peut-être a-t-il fallu éprouver d'abord—par quelle tendresse ou hantise insinuée?—la toute-puissance du néant, du vide, du désordre, de l'absence, pour parvenir à concevoir ces *actes absolus*, cette 'poésie absolue' et toutes ces irréfutables architectures destinées à contre-balancer l'absolu du *rien*. 'Je suis rapide ou rien.' C'est l'affirmation d'un esprit qui, pour exister, ne compte que sur sa propre agilité, sur la mobilité des perceptions créatrices, et sur l'exercice illimité de son pouvoir de rapt, dans le plus vaste déploiement d'une lucidité de proie. Mais cette affirmation est posée dans une alternative, et l'autre terme de l'alternative, c'est: rien. Tout acte se découpe ainsi sur un fond de néant. Mais cet acte sera une conquête, et d'abord une conquête de soi. Une conquête—ou un sauvetage: comme s'il fallait sauver l'équipage et la cargaison de quelque immense et permanent naufrage cosmique.

Jean Starobinski, 'Je suis rapide ou rien', in *Paul Valéry, Essais et Temoignages inédits*, ed. Marc Eigeldinger, Editions de la Baconnière, Neuchâtel, 1945, pp. 149–50.

Une photographie, récemment publiée dans un fascicule de la revue *Fontaine*, nous montre le poète assis sur un rocher au-dessus de la mer, le regard levé, brûlé dans le soleil et comme ivre, perdu dans l'étrange, c'est-à-dire dans le réel. Et ce réel, éclatant de blancheur, d'azur et d'or, tout entier visible et sensible, est cependant impénétrable. Le mystère y est présent et vivant en pleine lumière. Si Paul Valéry écarte délibérément toute espèce de pathos, il note d'autre part, dans un de ses cahiers: 'Angoisse, mon véritable métier.' Il y a un tragique de la pensée qui paraît en un certain point de ses entreprises. Et quand il considère le monde actuel, et sa folie, le tragique est dans son regard, dans le doute qu'il avoue, autant que dans la chose regardée.

Marcel Raymond, *Paul Valéry et la Tentation de l'Esprit*, Editions de la Baconnière, Neuchâtel, 1946, p. 7.

On a observé plus d'une fois que le style propre à Valéry, le plus proche du spontané, est extraordinairement accidenté. Partout, des ellipses et des tours personnels, des anacoluthes, des bonds par-dessus les idées intermédiaires, des parenthèses, guillemets, traits d'union ou de séparation. La pensée se débat dans le langage, le creuse; on dirait qu'elle ne lui est pas précisément consubstantielle, qu'elle éclate à travers lui, en quête de fissures, de points de moindre résistance. On a commenté, en particulier, le goût de l'écrivain pour les *italiques*. Les mots dont il se sert, il voudrait bien en restreindre ou en étendre la valeur, imposer ou suggérer un sens qui serait le sien, en telle circonstance, le seul nécessaire dans l'ordre de rapports où il se trouve.

Marcel Raymond, op. cit., p. 69.

Qu'on songe à cette observation de Montaigne: 'Qui suit un autre, il ne suit rien, il ne trouve rien, voire: il ne cherche rien', et à ce principe d'évaluation en matière d'éducation: 'Qu'il juge du profit qu'il aura fait, non par le témoignage de sa mémoire, mais de sa vie.' Ces principes ne sont-ils pas identiques à ceux qui ont commandé l'aventure intellectuelle de Valéry, son dédain de l'érudition, son souci de pousser toute connaissance jusqu'au réflexe?

André Berne-Joffroy, *Valéry*, Gallimard, 1960, p. 137.

He is too sceptical, too contemptuous of man in general, too penetrating perhaps, too hard an observer of the weak side of man; but also too indifferent to his yearnings and longings to be able to write with any conviction on political matters, closely allied as they are to the ethical requirements of man as a social being. For some reason or other, ever since Machiavelli was praised by Bacon for showing what human relations are instead of pointing at what they should be, a certain type of scientific or positivist student of man has endeavored to eliminate ethics from the world of men in society—as if the need most human beings feel for decency in behaviour were not a part of the picture in its own right as much as the rest. There is no denying the fact that Valéry is prone to take that point of view in his political writings. It leads him to strange utterances; nearly always coined with that clarity in design which is characteristic of his mint; nearly always also true and yet unsatisfactory, as either incomplete or too sweeping.

> Salvador de Madariaga, Introduction to Paul Valéry, *History and Politics, Collected Works of Paul Valéry*, Bollingen Foundation, 1962, pp. xxxiii–xxxiv.

Si on veut décrire le fonctionnement de l'esprit d'une façon exacte, on doit nécessairement tenir compte de l'existence chez l'homme d'un sentiment moral très réel, et souvent très fort, qui est une des marques les plus caractéristiques de sa vie intérieure. Toute analyse de l'esprit qui laisse ce sentiment de côté sera donc incomplète, et dans une certaine mesure, artificielle. Tel est malheureusement le cas de l'analyse de Valéry, qui semble tenir beaucoup plus à dénigrer les sentiments moraux en général qu'essayer d'en expliquer les origines et les rapports avec les autres aspects de notre activité psychique.

> Judith Robinson, *L'Analyse de l'Esprit dans les Cahiers de Valéry*, Corti, 1963, p. 190.

[On the garden-scene in Act II of 'Lust' of *Mon Faust*]: Five centuries before Valéry another Frenchman had found the supreme wisdom in living and knowing that one lives. Montaigne, too, had begun with a deep distrust of life and had first sought refuge in a proud and disdainful, Stoical withdrawal. He would have endorsed the remark Valéry had placed in the mouth of one of his early masks: 'Very well,' (said M. Teste.) 'The essential is against life.' But despite, or because of, his mature experience of many of the ills that assail the mind and body of man, Montaigne came at last to the conclusion that 'It is an absolute, an almost divine perfection, to know how rightly and truly to enjoy our existence.' The final conquest of this perfection was the ultimate masterpiece of the genius of Paul Valéry.

Lloyd James Austin, 'The Genius of Paul Valéry', in *Wingspread Lectures in the Humanities*, The Johnson Foundation, 1966, p. 55.

Une des particularités de la *Jeune Parque*, et qui explique son allure, doit être, en effet, cherchée dans l'intention de Valéry de contrarier systématiquement tout ce qui pourrait rappeler la prose et pas seulement dans la formulation si subtilement compliquée, mais aussi dans l'organisation du contenu imaginatif. C'est pourquoi il n'y a pas de récit, c'est pourquoi la chronologie de ces quelques heures de vie mentale est si étrangement bouleversée et oblige constamment le lecteur à revenir sur les pas de la Jeune Parque dans ses souvenirs, ses retours au présent, ses préfigurations de l'avenir. C'est pourquoi il n'y a pas de description, car comme le paysage, la peinture, elle a corrompu la littérature, et cette contrainte que s'est imposée Valéry est la cause de cette atmosphère, d'ailleurs si heureusement créée, où baigne l'héroïne du poème: c'est le lecteur, qui grâce à quelques suggestions, recrée tout le décor, où les grandes masses, ou plutôt les grandes puissances naturelles sont si présentes: le ciel, la mer, la terre, les étoiles, le soleil, et les détails pittoresques détachés comme des bijoux dans un écrin.

Jean Hytier, *Questions de Littérature*, Droz, 1967, p. 7.

Il ne faut jamais oublier qu'il y a pour Valéry *deux* langages tout à fait différents. Il y a d'abord le langage de l'analyse, qui est celui des *Cahiers*, et qui cherche constamment à se rapprocher du langage de la science et des mathématiques. C'est un langage qui veut être aussi précis que possible, où les mots sont rigoureusement définis, et où chaque terme, pour employer l'expression de Valéry, est *univoque*. Mais il y a d'autre part le langage de la poésie, qui est un langage volontairement imprécis, en ce sens que le poète fait exprès de le rendre ambigu ou *multivoque*, de manière à susciter chez le lecteur non pas une seule idée claire et distincte, mais une multiplicité d'idées, de prolongements intellectuels et de résonances affectives.

> Judith Robinson, [in a discussion after a paper by G. W. Ireland on *La Jeune Parque*] in *Entretiens sur Paul Valéry*, sous la direction de Emilie Noulet-Carner, Mouton, 1968, p. 106.

Valéry va, semble-t-il, beaucoup plus loin que Gide. Leur point de départ est à peu près le même; il s'agit ici et là, d'un culte du potentiel. Mais Gide va dans le sens du particulier, Valéry dans celui du moi pur... La différence capitale est que Valéry poursuit l'idée du potentiel, voire de *l'implexe*, jusqu'à ses ultimes conséquences, alors que Gide conclut à la nécessité de devenir à chaque instant tel ou tel, de développer le maximum possible de personnalités. Ajoutons que, pour Valéry il est impossible de réaliser effectivement son potentiel, de se définir à jamais par ses actes... Pour lui, on le voit, le moi *réel*, le moi *pur* échappe au contingent et donc à toute définition. Il est finalement ce que l'homme a de plus général, de moins *tel quel*. Ainsi s'explique la différence majeure entre le narcissisme de Valéry et celui de Gide; c'est celle qui distingue l'impersonnel du personnel.

> Margaret Mein, 'Valéry et Gide', in *Entretiens sur Paul Valéry*, sous la direction de Emilie Noulet-Carner, Mouton, 1968, pp. 194–5.

Précisons... ce qu'était le choix de Valéry parmi les classiques italiens: s'il estimait que Dante n'a rien donné aux Français, il aimait à entendre les sonnets de Pétrarque que lui lisait son ami Charles Du Bos et l'admirait particulièrement. En effet, il écrivait en 1922, dans une lettre à Jules Valéry, alors doyen de la faculté de droit à Montpellier, qui venait de faire un discours sur Pétrarque, ancien étudiant de droit à Montpellier: 'Pétrarque est un grand bonhomme. Il a tiré du sonnet presque tous ses effets et, à mon avis, c'est un père de la poésie française, par le XVIe qui en a extrait de quoi se tirer du genre naïf du XVe et rendre formel et musical ce qui était embarrassé, populaire ou roide etc.'

> Edmée de La Rochefoucauld, 'Paul Valéry et l'Italie', in *Entretiens sur Paul Valéry*, sous la direction de Emilie Noulet-Carner, Mouton, 1968, pp. 291–2.

La Soirée contient sa métaphore fonctionnelle, la clé de sa définitive contradiction, lorsque vers la fin Teste déclare: '*Je suis étant, et me voyant; me voyant me voir, et ainsi de suite.*' Nous sommes à l'opposé de Descartes, puisque le sujet cartésien, après le cogito, ne peut plus connaître de rupture décisive, tandis que l'expérience de Teste—l'expérience valéryenne—fait éclater toute présence du sujet: il faut que l'absence jaillisse de la présence même pour que la conscience apparaisse.

Jean Levaillant, 'Teste', in *Les Critiques de notre temps et Valéry*, ed. J. Bellemin-Noël, Garnier, 1971, p. 94.

'Il ne s'agit pas de maltraiter la littérature, écrit Blanchot, mais de chercher à la comprendre, et de voir pourquoi on ne la comprend qu'en la dépréciant.' Cette dépréciation, ou *dévaluation* salutaire, fut un des propos constants de Valéry, et l'on a peine à mesurer tout ce que la conscience et la pratique modernes de la littérature doivent à cet effort réducteur. Ce qui le rebute dans la littérature, c'est, comme il l'a souvent expliqué, le sentiment de l'*arbitraire*: 'Ce que je puis changer facilement m'offense chez moi, et m'ennuie chez les autres. D'où bien des conséquences anti-littéraires, et singulièrement anti-historiques.' Ou encore: 'Quant aux contes et à l'histoire, il m'arrive de m'y laisser prendre et de les admirer, comme excitants, passe-temps et ouvrages d'art; mais s'ils prétendent à la "vérité", et se flattent d'être pris au sérieux, l'arbitraire aussitôt et les conventions inconscientes se manifestent; et la manie perverse des substitutions possibles me saisit.' C'est évidemment cette manie, qu'il qualifie encore de *pratique détestable* et dont il avoue qu'elle *ruine des plaisirs*, qui lui rend tout à fait inconcevable l'art du récit, et le genre romanesque.

Gérard Genette, in *Les Critiques de notre temps et Valéry*, ed. J. Bellemin-Noël, Garnier, 1971, pp. 176–7.

L'actualité de Paul Valéry n'est plus à dire, ni sa modernité. Du moins comme théoricien, comme maître à penser, comme augure d'une certaine visée critique dans tous les secteurs de l'activité humaine, comme ce penseur qui a pressenti qu'il fallait réfléchir sur les formes et les structures plus que sur des éléments ou une substance, en s'inquiétant de trouver des 'modèles',—en cela il ouvrait la voie aux recherches tout à fait contemporaines. Homme axé sur l'avenir, homme presque du futur, expert à découvrir dans le passé et le présent ce que le présent et le passé ignorent être des germes.

Jean Bellemin-Noël, in *Matulu*, July–August 1971, p. 4.

Le titre de cette œuvre en 1895, *Introduction à la Méthode de Léonard de Vinci*, est révélateur. Ce n'est pas un livre sur Léonard, c'est un discours sur la Méthode. C'est un modèle au sens de modèle mécanique comme les Anglais en construisaient au XIXe siècle pour expliquer l'éther et les atomes, un modèle de fonctionnement. Valéry élabore une logique du modèle vingt ans avant les béhaviouristes et bien avant les structuralistes.

Janine Jallat, in *Matulu*, July–August 1971, p. 4.

NOTES
CHAPTER I: BIOGRAPHY

1. 'Le code rébarbatif et puant froid, les grises salles de cours où coule tristement l'éloquence juridique comme un robinet glacial dans une morgue . . .' *Lettres à Quelques-Uns*, p. 34 (1890).

2. A small number of his early poems, in revised form, can be read in the *Album de Vers Anciens*, published in 1920, (O.I, pp. 75–95), and the original versions of many early poems can be consulted (O.I, pp. 1530–1602).

3. Valéry's first contact with Wagner was in 1887 when he heard the prelude to *Lohengrin* in Montpellier. 'Quant à moi, je me réfère constamment à l'idée que je me fais de l'homme complet, ou plutôt de *l'action complète*, et considérant comme telle l'exécution d'une œuvre, mon 'idéal' est d'y voir concourir toutes nos forces et facultés. C'est pourquoi je fus si profondément conquis par ce qu'a fait Richard Wagner. . .' (Lettre à René Fernandat, 1944), O.II, p. 1538.

4. *André Gide – Paul Valéry, Correspondance* 1890–1942, ed. Robert Mallet, Gallimard, 1955. 'Gide, — nous sentons bien différemment les choses de l'esprit. Nous nous comprenons et nous nous savons admirablement. Par malheur, il croit que je le déprime, et je suis sûr qu'il m'excite. Je me suis aperçu que je ne le voyais pas comme ses amis le voient. Je vois Gide à peu près comme je me vois — c'est-à-dire qu'il me paraît digne de . . . justice. Ce mot abject n'a de sens qu'en égotisme. Saisissez s.v.p. Quand j'aime quelqu'un, je le traite comme moi-même, c'est-à-dire très mal, très soigneusement, très intimement durement. Je me rends insupportable — mais le sujet ne sait pas combien je parle, et je pense avec lui, avec quelle franchise! Cette franchise a été mon 'idéal' le plus cher. J'ai raconté cela à Gide il y a treize ou quatorze ans.' *Lettres à Quelques-Uns*, p. 67 (1905).

5. 'Puis-je faire comprendre en 1943 à quelques personnes beaucoup moins âgées que moi, l'effet que pouvait produire vers 1891 la rencontre brusque d'un certain jeune homme avec les vers de Mallarmé? Il faut supposer ce jeune homme assez occupé de poésie et sensible surtout aux inventions de forme, à la diversité des solutions qu'admet un vers, ayant par conséquent fort peu d'estime pour Lamartine ou pour Musset, ayant assez bien lu quelques Parnassiens, et observant dans Baudelaire le mélange plutôt déconcertant d'une magie extraordinaire, rebelle à toute analyse, et de parties détestables, expressions vulgaires et vers très

mauvais. J'insiste sur cette imperfection que je trouvais dans Baudelaire mêlée à une pleine puissance harmonique, car cette impression était comme expressément faite pour créer en moi le besoin, ou plutôt la *nécessité* de Mallarmé.

Dès le premier contact, et quel que fût l'effet premier d'obscurité et de complication de ses vers, il n'y eut en moi aucune hésitation sur l'importance exceptionnelle qu'il fallait consentir que leur existence prît en moi. Désormais, toutes autres poésies me semblèrent réduites à quantité de gauches tentatives, de fragments heureux, précédés ou suivis de morceaux insignifiants ou prosaïques. Je remarquais que les vers étranges du poète que je venais de découvrir avaient pour propriété singulière et première celle de se fixer d'eux-mêmes dans la mémoire. Ceci était particulièrement remarquable pour moi. Ma mémoire est d'une indiscipline déplorable. Je n'ai jamais pu apprendre une leçon par cœur. Or il arrivait que les vers de Mallarmé se fixaient d'eux-mêmes, sans le moindre effort, dans cette même mémoire.' (O.II, p. 1531).

6. Mr Harmut Köhler, of the University of Tübingen, is preparing a thesis on the problem of the relations between Mallarmé and Valéry. 'J'ai connu Mallarmé, *après* avoir subi son extrême influence, et au moment même où je guillotinais intérieurement la littérature.

J'ai adoré cet homme extraordinaire dans le temps même que j'y voyais la seule tête, hors de prix! — à couper, pour décapiter toute Rome. Vous sentez la passion qui peut exister dans un jeune monsieur de vingt-deux ans, fou de désirs contradictoires, incapable de les amuser; jaloux intellectuellement de toute idée qui lui semble comporter puissance et rigueur; amoureux non d'*âmes* — mais d'esprits et des plus divers, comme d'autres le sont des corps. . .' *Lettres à Quelques-Uns*, p. 95 (1912). The two letters to Albert Thibaudet (pp. 93–100), from which this passage is taken, are most important and should be consulted.

7. 'Celui qui m'a le plus fait sentir sa puissance fut Poe. J'y ai lu ce qu'il me fallait, pris ce délire de la lucidité qu'il communique.

Par conséquence, j'ai cessé de faire des vers. Cet art devenu impossible à moi de 1892, je le tenais déjà pour un exercice, ou application de recherches plus importantes.' *Lettres à Quelques-Uns*, p. 97 (1912).

8. 'Je ne me suis jamais référé qu'à mon MOI PUR, par quoi j'entends l'absolu de la conscience, qui est l'opération unique et uniforme de se dégager automatiquement de *tout*, et dans ce tout, figure notre personne même, avec son histoire, ses singularités, ses puissances diverses et ses complaissances propres.' *Lettres à Quelques-Uns* p. 245 (1943).

9. Here is Valéry's account of that important night:

'Nuit effroyable. Passée assis sur mon lit. Orage *partout*. Ma chambre éblouissante par chaque éclair. Et tout mon sort se jouait dans ma tête. Je suis entre moi et moi.

Nuit infinie. CRITIQUE. Peut-être effet de cette tension de l'air et de l'esprit. Et ces crevaisons violentes redoublées du ciel, ces illuminations brusques saccadées entre les murs purs de chaux nue.

Je me sens AUTRE ce matin. Mais — se sentir Autre — cela ne peut durer — soit que l'on *redevienne*; et que le premier l'emporte; soit que le nouvel homme absorbe et annule le premier.' (O.II, p. 1434)

'A l'âge de vingt ans, je fus contraint d'entreprendre une action très sérieuse contre les "Idoles" en général. Il ne s'agit d'abord que de l'une d'elles qui m'obséda, me rendit la vie presque insupportable. La force de l'absurde est incroyable. Quoi de plus humiliant pour l'esprit que tout le mal que fait ce rien : une image, un élément mental destiné à l'oubli ?

. . .

Cette crise me dressa contre ma "sensibilité" en tant qu'elle entreprenait sur la liberté de mon esprit. J'essayai, sans grand succès immédiat, d'opposer la conscience de mon état à cet état lui-même, et l'observateur au patient.

. . .

Tout ceci me conduisit à décréter toutes les Idoles *hors la loi*. Je les immolai toutes à celle qu'il fallut bien créer pour lui soumettre les autres, *l'Idole de l'Intellect*; de laquelle mon *Monsieur Teste* fut le grand-prêtre.' (O.II, pp. 1510–11)

10. In the first number of the *Mercure de France* in 1890, Alfred Vallette had declared: 'Nous opposerons à la désolante et universelle négation cette affirmation résolue: MOI.'

11. *Correspondance Gide-Valéry*, p. 182 (1893).

12. 'Ayant bien vu et trouvé *pour moi* vers la vingtième année que l'homme est un système fermé quant à la connaissance et aux actes — que le "*Que peut un homme?*" de M. Teste devint toute ma philosophie.' (O.II, p. 1518).

13. 'Le monde est plein d'intelligentes mollesses. Et qui a du courage doit perdre les meilleures années à se refaire entièrement le cerveau.' *Correspondance Gide-Valéry*, p. 215 (1894).

14. See *Correspondance Paul-Valéry – Gustave Fourment*, ed. Octave Nadal, Gallimard, 1957, pp. 145–51 (1898), for Valéry's own description of his research.

15. 'Plus je vais, plus je me sens esclave du physique . . .', *Correspondance Gide-Valéry*, p. 374 (1900).

16. Christine Crow, *Paul Valéry, Consciousness and Nature*, Cambridge University Press, 1972, p. 52.

17. 'Citer quelques écrits, ayant plus de douze syllabes, produits sans nul secours de la raison, et ne faisant en aucun point regretter cette absence.' *Lettres à Quelques-Uns*, p. 113 (1916).

18. In a letter to Huysmans, Valéry explains his interest in the mystics:

'Je découvre en eux les plus grands maîtres d'une méthode d'investig-
ation qui me hante — celle qui consiste à imaginer, à laisser faire le
travail spirituel avec toute son ampleur et même son apparente absurdité
fantastique . . .' *Lettres à Quelques-Uns*, p. 54 (1895). In *Propos Me Concernant*, he comments on his lack of "anxiété métaphysique": 'Plusieurs ont
cru devoir m'attribuer je ne sais quelle "anxiété métaphysique". Je
connais malheureusement assez l'anxiété; qui est un détestable état. Je
voudrais bien que ce tourment de mes nerfs eût pour "cause" quelque
question de métaphysique: j'en ferais mon affaire. Mais je ne m'arrête
jamais sur des problèmes dont il est si facile de voir que leurs énoncés ne
sont que des abus du langage — et leur solutions celles que l'on veut.'
O.II, p. 1536. Cf. also 'Je ne suis pas l'homme de Dieu ni de la campagne,'
Correspondance Gide-Valéry, p. 255 (1896).

19. 'La production d'idées est chez moi une fonction naturelle, quasi
physiologique — dont l'empêchement m'est une véritable gêne de mon
régime physique, et dont l'écoulement m'est nécessaire. — Je suis
positivement malade tout le jour si je n'ai pu, à peine réveillé, pendant
deux heures environ, me laisser faire par ma tête'. *Propos Me Concernant*,
O.II, p. 1526.

20. *L'Arche*, October 1945, p. 14.

21. In 1915, Valéry wrote to André Fontainas about this article:
'Admettons que cet écrit eût été précis — vrai, etc. Demandez-vous
maintenant quelles suites pratiques il eût pu avoir en notre bienheureux
pays dans les années 1897 à 1914?

. . .

Mais ici, rien à faire. Impotence radicale (ou radicale-socialiste).

Il en résulte donc, que . . . notre système que vous voyez là triomphe
des initiatives individuelles . . .' *Lettres à Quelques-Uns*, p. 111.

22. A few days after the death of Mallarmé, Valéry wrote to Gide:
'Cela me soulagera un peu d'écrire, car il y a trois nuits que je ne dors
plus, que je pleure comme un enfant et que j'étouffe.' *Correspondance
Gide-Valéry*, p. 331 (1898). Although Valéry had very little money, he
assisted Mallarmé's widow and daughter financially on a regular basis,
aided by contributions from Gide and Viélé-Griffin.

23. 'Tu penses bien que *mon* travail est impossible après une journée de
siège et de plume.' *Correspondance Valéry-Fourment*, p. 154 (1900).

24. Still, in 1903 he complains of interruptions and intellectual solitude:
'Ce qui m'éreinte, c'est l'interruption infinie de mes occupations. Je
prends, je quitte, — je me désole bêtement (car enfin tout cela est peu de
chose). Ma journée est toute brisée.

Enfin, il faut aussi que pour moi seul, je garde terriblement ma pensée.
Nul ne peut à loisir la comprendre ni surtout la contredire.' *Correspondance Valéry-Fourment*, pp. 172–3 (1903).

25. 'Cet homme me plaît infiniment, autant que sa peinture.' *Correspondance Gide-Valéry*, p. 260 (1896).

26. Valery resisted the idea of publishing a collection of his verse and prose: 'Publier ce que j'ai fait, est-ce pas consacrer l'abandon et la catastrophe de ce pour quoi j'avais abandonné ce que j'ai fait?' *Correspondance Gide-Valéry*, p. 426. He was, however, clearly worried about his financial future: 'Je puis me trouver *demain* dans une situation très embarrassante et je me dis, malgré tout, que peut-être un livre paru, alors, me servirait un peu.' *Correspondance Gide-Valéry*, p. 428 (1912). Valéry *may* have published a new version of his early poem, 'Orphée', in September 1913. See H. A. Grubbs, *Paul Valéry*, Twayne, 1968 pp. 43–4.

27. 'Je regarde la poésie comme le genre le moins idolâtre. Elle est le *sport* des hommes insensibles aux valeurs fiduciaires du langage commun, et qui ne spéculent pas sur cette falsification que l'on nomme *vérité*, ou *nature*.

Je viens de prononcer le mot *sport*. C'est que je rapporte tout ce que je pense de l'art à l'idée d'*exercice*, que je trouve la plus belle idée du monde ... C'est le grand art pour moi en matière de poésie que de dresser l'animal *Langage*, et de le mener où il n'a pas coutume d'aller; mais de l'y mener avec l'apparence de la liberté la plus dégagée. Il s'agit de conquérir cette liberté, de la pousser jusqu'à la grâce; et, non seulement tout effort vers cette perfection profite à la beauté et à la durée intrinsèque de l'ouvrage, mais elle transforme en retour l'auteur même en quelqu'un de plus indépendant à l'égard des mots, c'est-à-dire, plus maître de sa pensée.' *Propos Me Concernant*, O.II, p. 1530.

28. 'Les 23 ans et plus dépensés à maintes analyses, les transformations intérieures créées ou adoptées à leur intention, n'ont pas peu contribué, quand je suis revenu à la poésie, à m'en faire pénétrer certaines finesses. J'ai employé, si vous supportez cette image, des appareils cent et mille fois plus précis à observer *la même chose* que j'observais en 1891.' *Lettres à Quelques-Uns*, pp. 131–2 (1919). See also in *Lettres à Quelques-Uns*, pp. 115–18 where there are comments on the final verses of *La Jeune Parque* and on the title. Also pp. 122–5 where he mentions the War: 'Qui croirait que tels vers ont été écrits dans ce temps par un homme suspendu aux "Communiqués", la pensée à Verdun et ne cessant d'y penser?' p. 123. The same letter has an important passage on the benefits he received from writing the poem: 'Je puis dire en passant, que le véritable bénéfice tiré par moi de cette *Parque*, réside dans des observations sur moi-même prises pendant le travail.' Pp. 123–4. The same letter describes the subject of the poem: 'Le sujet vague de l'œuvre est la Conscience de soi-même...' p. 124. See also p. 130: 'Je vous avoue que je ne m'attendais pas à cette faveur qui accueille, ici et là, mes derniers vers. Je les ai faits de mon mieux, mais en dehors des occupations du siècle et des gens du siècle;

comme un devoir vis-à-vis de grandes choses, ou mourantes, ou mortes.'
See also pp. 143–5 and 178–81 for more letters on *La Jeune Parque*.

29. Success, however, often exasperated Valéry: 'Rencontré Paul
Valéry chez Adrienne Monnier. L'ai longuement raccompagné. Il se
dit gêné, exaspéré même par la fausse situation où le porte son succès.'
Correspondance Gide-Valéry, p. 494, note 2 (from Gide's *Journal*, 30 December
1922). Again, in 1926: 'Je suis fatigué d'être la proie d'autrui', p. 504.
Already in 1917, soon after publication of *La Jeune Parque*, Valéry had
written to Pierre Louÿs: 'Oh! rester dans le réversible!' *Lettres à Quelques-
Uns*, p. 120.

30. M. Bémol, *Paul Valéry*, G. de Bussac, 1949, p. 308. Cf. 'Il est cinq
heures et le jour est encore nuit. Je n'ai que ce moment que j'aime, pour
être moi. Le reste est livré aux gens, au travail *extérieur*, au désordre
irrésistible et diabolique de Paris.' *Lettres à Quelques-Uns*, p. 191 (1930).

31. André Gide, *Journal*, 1889–1939, Bibliothèque de la Pléiade, p.
949. A letter to Jean de Latour in 1933 has a similar sentence: 'Je n'ai
jamais écrit en prose que sur demande ou commande, — *sujet* imposé
et, parfois, conditions bizarres.' O.II, p. 1499. Valéry would have preferred not to publish at all: 'J'ai bien rarement l'idée de faire un livre.
C'est un besoin que je ressens fort peu: répandre et faire partager ma
pensée ne m'excite guère. Pensez comme vous voudrez! Cependant, à
plus d'une reprise, me séduisit l'idée de composer une manière de
Traité de l'entraînement de l'esprit. Je l'appelais *Gladiator* du nom d'un
célèbre cheval de course . . . J'en ai quantité d'éléments.' *Propos Me
Concernant*, O.II, p. 1530. Valéry did, however, find the 'imposed' subjects
stimulating for his mind: 'Quoi de plus fécond que l'imprévu pour la
pensée?

C'est pourquoi je me suis fait à accepter ces besognes non projetées que
j'ai accomplies par centaines.' *Propos Me Concernant*, O.II, p. 1523.

32. 'J'aime M. de Stendhal parce qu'il écrit comme on *se* parle —
c'est-à-dire comme je me parle souvent. Et il est si raisonnable. Par
ailleurs, c'est presque le *seul* écrivain dont je supporte les passages
d'amour.' *Correspondance Gide-Valéry*, p. 291 (1897).

33. 'Plus j'y songe et plus c'est VRAI: il y a dans l'amitié toutes les
ressources, *toutes*, pour chez une élite, user définitivement la notion
Amour, la remplacer. Considère la conception d'une communication
mieux qu'illusoire entre deux êtres, comme la limite ou circonférence
du problème et vois combien l'approché amical surpasse l'érotique.'
Correspondance Valéry-Fourment, pp. 132–3 (1892). 'J'ai fréquenté tous mes
amis dans le dessein de leur offrir quelque jour une suprême fiançaille,
une expérience d'apothéose.' Ibid., p. 134 (1893). 'J'ai peu à peu dû
renoncer à cette culture des amitiés qui jusqu'à ces 3 ou 4 dernières
années a pris les 2/3 de ma vie — et de laquelle je me félicite encore. Je

me dis souvent: combien de bons compagnons j'ai rencontrés — quelle chance — grâce à des esprits comme tel et tel (le tien) j'ai su tout de suite — ou très tôt chercher les vraies valeurs, ne pas avoir confiance dans celui qui imprime, est lu ou connu.

Par inversion, j'ai vu nettement le défaut de l'écrit — sa fausseté — (s'adresser à un public *vague*). J'ai senti qu'il était une dégradation, un abaissement de la chose fine et toujours profonde, constituée entre soi, *ad amicum*, élégance suprême. Mais je m'avoue que je n'ai pas réussi — dans aucun cas — à pousser *extrêmement loin* le voisinage spirituel.' Ibid., p. 157 (1900). 'J'aurais voulu trouver qui eût été avec moi comme je suis avec moi.' Ibid., p. 158 (1900). 'Maintenant . . . je me suis peu à peu élaboré des goûts si particuliers, — une manière de penser si élémentaire ou singulière — je vois le monde si à ma façon — que j'ai renoncé à toute particularité communicable — je me tiens, *dès qu'il y a quelqu'un*, dans la normale. C'est-à-dire que je ne fais plus d'amitiés.' Ibid., p. 158 (1900). 'Je sais que l'amitié aura été ma grande passion. Je hais public, foule, et humanité à proportion du goût que j'éprouve pour les coteries et les quelques-uns. Je n'ai pas à me plaindre. J'ai été heureux en amis.' Ibid., p. 169 (1903).

34. 'Je m'assure . . . que l'ingénuité et le feu paraissent dans l'homme vers les cinquante ans. A ce point de la vie, il ne vaut plus la peine de calculer; la prévoyance devient vaine et son objet *imaginaire*; la sagacité, absurde; la prudence ridicule; et l'on peut se consumer sans regret comme il est temps de se consumer sans retard. Rien de plus chaud ni de plus naïf que cet âge.' From *Au Lecteur*, pp. i–iv in Maurice Courtois-Suffit, *Le Promeneur Sympathique, Avec quelques mots de Paul Valéry*, L'Aubier, Collection de romans et d'essais, Librairie Plon, 1925. In O.II, p. 1490.

35. The Collège de France, founded by Francis I and separate from the university system, offers lecture courses to the general public in a variety of fields, given by the most eminent specialists. These specialists are elected by the other professors, and the chair is created specifically for the individual. We know what Valéry said in his lectures at the Collège de France through notes made by Georges Le Breton and published in *Yggdrasill*, 25 December 1937–25 February 1939.

36. 'Il résulte de tout ceci que les hommes qui, comme moi, tiennent sur toute chose à l'esprit, et *d'autre part*, abhorrent la guerre, doivent agir contre la guerre par les voies de l'esprit, — et je n'entends pas par ces mots désigner les harangues, les déclamations, les résolutions de meetings, les serments, etc., car ce sont des actes de violence, qui n'excluent pas l'*âme de guerre*, s'ils semblent condamner la chose. La guerre naît de la politique; la politique, quelle qu'elle soit, a besoin pour ses fins de la crédulité, de l'excitabilité, de l'émotivité; il lui faut de l'indignation, de la haine, de la confiance, des mirages, — et ce sont là autant de moyens

de changer l'homme en animal de combat. Il ne vaut pas la peine de songer à abolir les guerres, si l'on ne s'occupe en profondeur à éliminer la bestialité.' *Lettres à Quelques-Uns*, pp. 201–2 (1932).

CHAPTER II: POETRY

Early Poetry

1. This section first appeared in the *Australian Journal of French Studies*.

2. See James R. Lawler, 'Existe! . . . Sois enfin toi-même', *Australian Journal of French Studies*, viii, 1971, pp. 151–2.

3. *Correspondance de Paul Valéry et de Gustave Fourment*, ed. Octave Nadal, Gallimard, 1957, p. 134 (letter dated February 1893).

4. Cf. 'Viol', O.I, p. 1577, written in 1890: 'une coupable et triste et trop exquise étreinte', where it is the woman who rapes a young boy.

5. See Jean Bellemin-Noël, 'Le Narcissisme des "Narcisse" (Valéry)', *Littérature*, May 1972, p. 39.

6. Compare these lines from 'Narcisse Parle' with the same lines, slightly modified, in 'Fragments du Narcisse', where the decor has become more intimately linked to Narcissus:

> J'entends les herbes d'or grandir dans l'ombre sainte
> Et la lune perfide élève son miroir
> Si la fontaine claire est par la nuit éteinte!
>
> . . .
>
> J'entends l'herbe des nuits croître dans l'ombre sainte,
> Et la lune perfide élève son miroir
> Jusque dans les secrets de la fontaine éteinte . . .

7. This and subsequent quotations are from Valéry's elaborate early draft of the poem, revealed by Lawler's article cited in note 2.

La Jeune Parque

8. *La Jeune Parque*, ed. Nadal, Club du Meilleur Livre, Paris, 1957, pp. 221 and 222.

9. *Athalie*, Act II, scene 5. *Esther*, Act I, scene 4.

10. Nadal, op. cit., Facsimile VI/44.

11. Jacques Duchesne-Guillemin, *Etudes pour un Paul Valéry*, A la Baconnière, Neuchâtel, 1964, pp. 65–6.

12. Ibid., p. 45.

13. Nadal, op. cit., p. 82.

14. Duchesne-Guillemin, op. cit., p. 181.

15. Lucienne Julien Cain, *Trois Essais sur Paul Valéry*, Gallimard, 1958, p. 94.

16. Hans Sorensen, *La Poésie de Paul Valéry, Etude Stylistique sur La Jeune Parque*, Arnold Busck, Copenhagen, 1954, p. 243.

Charmes

17. Readers may consult *Charmes ou Poèmes*, ed. C. G. Whiting, The Athlone Press, 1973, pp. 48–52, which reproduces the 1922 version of the first section of the poem.

18. Jacques Duchesne-Guillemin, *Etude de Charmes*, L'Ecran du Monde, 1947, p. 57.

19. See *Cahiers* II, pp. 534–5.

CHAPTER III: POETICS

1. W. N. Ince, *The Poetic Theory of Paul Valéry*, Leicester University Press, 1961, p. 115.

2. Frédéric Lefèvre, *Une heure avec Paul Valéry*. Quoted in J. Hytier, *La Poétique de Valéry*, Armand Colin, 1953, pp. 215–16.

3. 'Réponse', in *Commerce*, Summer 1932, p. 13. Quoted in J. Hytier, op. cit., p. 298, n. 2.

4. 'La littérature comme telle' in *Figures*, Editions du Seuil, 1966.

5. 'Je ne puis séparer mon idée de la poésie de celle de formations *achevées* — qui se suffisent, dont le son et les effets psychiques se répondent, avec un certain 'indéfiniment'. Alors quelque chose est détachée, comme un fruit ou enfant, de sa génération et du possible qui baigne l'esprit — et s'oppose à la mutabilité des pensées et à la liberté du langage-fonction. Ce qui s'est produit et affirmé ainsi n'est plus de *quelqu'un*, mais comme la manifestation de propriétés intrinsèques, impersonnelles, de la fonction composée *Langage* — se dégageant rarement, dans des conditions aussi rarement réunies que celles qui font le carbone diamant —.' (*Cahiers* II, p. 1135)

6. Cited by Ince, op. cit., p. 85 n. 4.

7. Pierre Guiraud, *Langage et Versification d'après l'œuvre de Paul Valéry*, Klincksieck, 1953, p. 155.

8. *Paul Valéry Vivant*, Cahiers du Sud, 1946, p. 224, and 'Svedenborg', O.I, p. 875.

9. Albert Henry, *Langage et Poésie chez Paul Valéry*, Mercure de France, 1952.

10. These conventions, however, must never become merely mechanical: 'Le vers régulier est *bon* quand il donne l'idée d'une improbabilité de plus — d'une coincidence encore *plus* merveilleuse. Il éloigne dans le cas contraire – quand il apporte sa part de facilité, ou de mécanisme automatique . . .' (*Cahiers* II, p. 1063).

11. Ince, op. cit., chapter 4.

12. ' "Création artistique". La création par l'artiste — dans sa phase spontanée, réflexe — me semble être comparable à une reprise d'équilibre ou à l'envahissement d'un vase par un gaz. Il y a un certain *vide* qui demande, appelle — ce *vide* peut être plus ou moins déterminé — ce peut être un certain rythme, — une figure-contour, — une question — un état — un temps devant moi, — un outil, une page blanche, une surface murale, un terrain ou emplacement.' (*Cahiers* II, p. 1018)

13. Christine Crow, *Paul Valéry, Consciousness and Nature*, Cambridge University Press, 1972, pp. 184–97.

CHAPTER IV: SEVEN PROSE WORKS

'*La Soirée avec Monsieur Teste*'

1. See O.II, pp. 11–75 and 1375–6, also 'Teste' and 'Soirée avec Monsieur Teste' in the index of *Cahiers* II.

2. J. A. E. Loubère, 'Balzac: Le grand absent de chez Teste,' *French Review*, Special issue 6, 1974, pp. 82–91.

3. '*M. Teste, Léonard*, peignent de leur mieux les ambitions de mes 25 ans.' *Lettres à Quelques-Uns*, Gallimard, 1952, p. 133.

4. See l. 35, *La Jeune Parque*: 'Je me voyais me voir, sinueuse. . .'

5. 'Je tends par ma nature à négliger tout ce que ma nature trouve sans conséquence pour son accroissement permanent propre, — les choses que j'appelle *accidents* ou *cas particuliers*. Je dis *ma nature* car j'ai observé que ma mémoire ne retient pas certaines choses et ne peut oublier certaines autres. Elle est un tri automatique. Elle a sans doute ses raisons...

Or, qu'oublie-t-elle? Ce qui pourrait être tout autre, sans inconvénient pour l'action intérieure de moi en moi sur moi.

Elle garde ce qui peut m'être utile pour lutter contre les monstres intimes, et pour former un être instantané plus libre c'est-à-dire pourvu de plus de doutes efficaces, de plus de solutions disponibles. Beaucoup de *modèles* et peu de *documents*. Je suis antihistorique. Mon mouvement est généralement une *défense par changement d'axes* et de *nombre de dimensions*. Je me cherche toujours un degré de plus de liberté d'esprit . . .' (O.II, pp. 1529–30). (See also the *Cahier* chapter on *Mémoire*.)

6. 'Autre trait: je ne vois pas ce qui est autour de moi; je n'ai besoin d'aucun décor, et c'est dans une chambre d'hôtel, aussi impersonnelle que possible, que je travaille le plus volontiers. Mais si quelque objet me requiert, mes yeux le creusent et l'épuisent. En quelque sorte, il me semble que *je fais plus que le voir en le regardant*.' (O.II, pp. 1534–5.)

7. Valéry noted in 1928 that 'les réunions d'humains . . . me font toujours un étrange effet'. Cited in H. Laurenti, *Paul Valéry et le théâtre*, Gallimard, 1973, p. 131.

8. H. Laurenti, 'Paul Valéry en son temps', *Europe*, July 1971, p. 7.

9. *Cahiers* I, p. 316. The name 'Teste' evokes not only 'tête' and 'témoin', but also 'testicule'.

10. This is Hackett's interpretation of 'la bêtise' in the famous first line of 'La Soirée'. See C. A. Hackett, 'Teste et la Soirée avec Monsieur Teste', *French Studies*, April 1967, pp. 111–24.

11. 'Ça ne va pas du tout. Je suis dans les névralgies, les insomnies et tout le tremblement. J'ai passé des nuits atroces. Je ne sais si c'est le temps ou autre chose, mais tout ce mois m'a été bien dur.' *Correspondance Gide-Valéry*, Gallimard, 1955, p. 275 (1896).

'Introduction à la Méthode de Léonard de Vinci'

12. 'Ma conviction, dès la jeunesse, fut que, dans la phase la plus vivante de la recherche intellectuelle, il n'y a pas de différence, autre que nominale, entre les manœuvres intérieures d'un artiste ou poète, et celles d'un savant, — en les prenant, l'un et l'autre, bien entendu, parmi ceux qui placent leur désir au-dessus de toute carrière. . . Je crois encore qu'à haute température, les spécialités s'effacent assez.' *Lettres à Quelques-Uns*, Gallimard, 1952, p. 241 (1943).

13. See F. E. Sutcliffe, *La Pensée de Paul Valéry*, Nizet, 1955, p. 173.

14. Sutcliffe, ibid, pp. 76–88, and Pierre Laurette, *Le Thème de l'Arbre chez Paul Valéry*, Klincksieck, 1967, pp. 97–101. See also Reino Virtanen, 'Paul Valéry's Scientific Education', *Symposium*, Winter 1973, pp. 362–378.

'L'Ame et la Danse'

15. Paul Valéry, *Eupalinos and L'Ame et la Danse*, ed. Vera Daniel, Oxford University Press, 1967. Jacques Duchesne-Guillemin, 'L'Ame et la Danse Revisitées', *French Studies*, October 1969, pp. 362–77.

L'Idée Fixe

16. Judith Robinson, 'Words and Silence in 'L'Idée Fixe', *Modern Language Notes*, vol. 87, no. 4, May 1972, p. 653, note 38.

17. See, for example, 'Note et Digression' (O.I, pp. 1199–233), and in *Charmes*, 'Ebauche d'un Serpent'.

Mon Faust

18. 'Quand on est enfant on se *découvre*, on découvre lentement l'espace de son corps, on exprime la particularité de son corps par une série d'efforts, je suppose? On se tord et on se trouve ou on se retrouve, et on s'étonne! on touche son talon, on saisit son pied droit avec sa main gauche, on obtient le pied froid dans la paume chaude! . . . Maintenant, je me sais par cœur. Le cœur aussi. Bah! toute la terre est marquée, tous les pavillons couvrent tous les territoires.' (O.II, p. 24.)

19.   'Les dieux m'ont-ils formé ce maternel contour
             Et ces bords sinueux, ces plis et ces calices,
             Pour que la vie embrasse un autel de délices,
             Où mêlant l'âme étrange aux éternels retours,
             La semence, le lait, le sang coulent toujours?'
                                                  (ll. 260–4)

20. 'Je suis né, à vingt ans, exaspéré par la répétition — c'est-à-dire
contre la vie... Je ne pouvais que mon esprit ne voulût toujours "passer
à la limite" — brûler tout ce qu'il re-connaissait — à peine reconnu.
L'amour me paraissait redites; tout le "sentiment" enregistré depuis des
siècles. "*Je t'aime*' impossible à dire sans que l'on perdît sa raison d'être,
d'*Etre d'une seule fois.*" (*Cahiers*, I, pp. 175–6.)

21. 'Je n'aime rien tant que ce qui va se produire; et jusque dans
l'amour je ne trouve rien qui l'emporte en volupté sur les tout premiers
sentiments.' 'L'Ame et la Danse' (O.II, p. 159).

CHAPTER VI: CAHIERS

1. 'Nietzsche excitait en moi la combativité de l'esprit, et le plaisir
enivrant de la promptitude des *réponses* que j'ai toujours un peu trop
goûté. Il me plaisait aussi par le vertige intellectuel de l'excès de conscience et de relations pressenties, par certains *passages à la limite*, par la
présence d'une volonté supérieure intervenant pour se créer les obstacles
et les exigences sans lesquels la pensée ne sait que se fuir. J'y remarquais
je ne sais quelle intime alliance du lyrique et de l'analytique que nul
encore n'avait aussi délibérément accomplie. Enfin, dans le jeu de cette
idéologie nourrie de musique, j'appréciais fort le mélange et l'usage très
heureux de notions et de données d'origine savante; Nietzsche était
comme armé de philologie et de physiologie combinées, remarquable-
ment adaptées ou associées à son mécanisme mental.

Mais il me choquait par d'autres endroits. Il irritait en moi le sentiment de la rigueur. Je ne concevais pas que ce violent et vaste esprit n'en
eût pas fini avec l'invérifiable...' *Quatre Lettres de Paul Valéry au sujet de
Nietzsche*, Cahiers de la Quinzaine, 1927, pp. 11–13. See also: E. Gaède,
Nietzsche et Valéry, Gallimard 1962.

CHAPTER VII: LITERARY FORTUNES AND
INFLUENCE

1. T. S. Eliot, 'Dante', in *The Sacred Wood*, Methuen, 1920, p. 170.
2. Ibid., pp. 171, 170. See James Lawler, *The Poet as Analyst*,
University of California Press, 1974, pp. 282–306.

3. T. S. Eliot, 'From Poe to Valéry', *The Hudson Review*, Autumn 1949, p. 339.

4. T. S. Eliot, Introduction to *The Art of Poetry*, vol. vii, *Collected Works of Paul Valéry*, The Bollingen Foundation, Pantheon, 1958, p. xvii. (The American poet, Wallace Stevens, who was very familiar with the poetry of Baudelaire, Mallarmé and Valéry, wrote two prefaces for volume iv of this series, *Dialogues*, 1956. For two views of possible links between Stevens and Valéry, see Michel Benamou, *Wallace Stevens and the Symbolist Imagination*, Princeton 1972, and the 1975 Princeton University doctoral dissertation by Merle Zena Ruberg, 'Paul Valéry and Wallace Stevens: their poetry and poetics'.)

5. T. S. Eliot, 'Leçon de Valéry', in *Paul Valéry Vivant*, Cahiers du Sud, 1946, pp. 74–81.

6. Ibid., p. 74.

7. Ibid., p. 78.

8. T. S. Eliot, Foreword to Joseph Chiari, *Contemporary French Poetry*, Philosophical Library, 1952, p. x.

9. T. S. Eliot, Introduction to *The Art of Poetry*, p. xix.

10. T. S. Eliot, Introduction to *Le Serpent*, Criterion, 1924, p. 12.

11. Ibid., pp. 12–13.

12. Rainer Maria Rilke, 'Fragments sur Valéry', in *Paul Valéry Vivant* Cahiers du Sud, 1946, p. 217.

13. Judith Ryan, 'Creative Subjectivity in Rilke and Valéry', *Comparative Literature*, Winter 1973, pp. 1–16.

14. Jorge Guillén, *Language and Poetry*, Harvard 1961, p. 209.

15. Gérard Genette, 'La Littérature comme telle', in *Figures*, Editions du Seuil, 1966, pp. 253–65.

16. J. A. E. Loubère, 'Borges and the "wicked" thoughts of Paul Valéry', *Modern Fiction Studies*, Autumn 1973, pp. 419–31.

17. Ibid., p. 428.

18. André Breton, *Entretiens*, Gallimard, 1952, p. 15.

19. H. S. Gershman, 'Valéry and Breton', *Yale French Studies*, no.44, pp. 199–206.

20. E. Gaède, Review of *Yale French Studies*, no. 44, *R.H.L.F.*, Sept.–Oct. 1973, p. 921.

21. Laurent Le Sage, 'Valéry and Sartre', *Modern Language Quarterly*, June 1971, p. 196.

22. Tzvetan Todorov, 'Valéry's Poetics', *Yale French Studies*, no.44, pp. 65–72.

23. Gérard Genette, op. cit., pp. 253–65.

24. Jacques Derrida, 'Les Sources de Valéry', *Modern Language Notes*, May 1972, pp. 563–99.

25. Nicole Celeyrette-Pietri, 'Le Jeu du je', in *Paul Valéry Contemporain*, Klincksieck, 1974, pp. 11–25.

26. Ibid., p. 25.

27. Jean Ricardou, ' "Casseur" et "Poète d'Etat" ', *Le Figaro Littéraire*, July 13–19, 1970, p. 22.

28. Ibid., p. 23.

SELECT BIBLIOGRAPHY

WORKS BY PAUL VALERY

Paul Valéry, *Œuvres* I and II, ed. Jean Hytier, Bibliothèque de la Pléiade, 1957 and 1960.

The Collected Works of Paul Valéry (ed. J. Matthews) vols i–xv, Princeton University Press, The Bollingen Foundation, 1956–75.

Paul Valéry, *Cahiers* I and II, ed. Judith Robinson, Bibliothèque de la Pléiade, 1973 and 1974.

La Jeune Parque, ed. Octave Nadal, Le Club du Meilleur Livre, 1957.

Charmes ou Poèmes, ed. Charles G. Whiting, Athlone French Poets, Athlone Press, 1973.

Eupalinos and L'Ame et la Danse, ed. Vera Daniel, Oxford, 1967.

Lettres à Quelques-Uns, Gallimard, 1952.

Correspondance André Gide - Paul Valéry, ed. Robert Mallet, Gallimard, 1955.

Correspondance Paul Valéry - Gustave Fourment, ed. Octave Nadal, Gallimard 1957.

WORKS ON PAUL VALERY

Lloyd James Austin, 'The Genius of Paul Valéry', Wingspread Lectures in the Humanities, The Johnson Foundation, 1966.

Ned Bastet, *La Symbolique des Images dans l'Œuvre Poétique de Valéry*, Faculté des Lettres — Aix-en-Provence, Travaux et Mémoires XXIV, 1962.

Jean Bellemin-Noël (ed.), *Les Critiques de notre temps et Valéry*, Garnier, 1971.

Maurice Bémol, *Paul Valéry*, G. de Bussac, 1949.

André Berne-Joffroy, *Valéry*, Gallimard, 1960.

Lucienne Cain, *Trois Essais sur Paul Valéry*, Gallimard, 1958.

Christine Crow, *Paul Valéry: Consciousness and Nature*, Cambridge University Press, 1972.

André Dabezies, *Visages de Faust au XXe siecle*, Presses Universitaires de France, 1967.

Jacques Duchesne-Guillemin, *Etudes pour un Paul Valéry*, La Baconnière, 1964.

Entretiens sur Paul Valéry, sous la direction de Emilie Noulet-Carner, Mouton, 1968.

Edouard Gaède, *Nietzsche et Valéry*, Gallimard, 1962.

Albert Henry, *Langage et Poésie chez Paul Valéry*, Mercure de France, 1952.

Jean Hytier, *La Poétique de Valéry*, A. Colin, 1953.

W. N. Ince, *The Poetic Theory of Paul Valéry*, Leicester University Press, 1970.

James Lawler, *Lecture de Valéry*, Presses Universitaires de France, 1963.

James Lawler, *The Poet as Analyst, Essays on Paul Valéry*, University of California Press, 1974.

Huguette Laurenti, *Paul Valéry et le théâtre*, Gallimard 1973.

Pierre Laurette, *Le Thème de l'arbre chez Paul Valéry*, Klincksieck, 1967.

Monique Maka-De Schepper, *Le Thème de la Pythie chez Paul Valéry*, Société d'édition 'Les Belles Lettres', 1969.

Emilie Noulet, *Paul Valéry*, La Renaissance du Livre, 1951.

Monique Parent, *Cohérence et Résonance dans le style de Charmes*, Klincksieck 1970.

François Pire, *La Tentation du sensible chez Paul Valéry*, La Renaissance du Livre, 1964.

Paul Valéry Contemporain, Actes et Colloques no. 12, Klincksieck, 1974.

Paul Valéry: Essais et Témoignages inédits, ed. Marc Eigeldinger, La Baconnière, 1945.

Paul Valéry, Lectures de Charmes, sous la direction de Huguette Laurenti, *La Revue des Lettres Modernes*, no. 413–18, 1974.

Paul Valéry Vivant, Cahiers du Sud, 1946.

Marcel Raymond, *Paul Valéry et la tentation de l'esprit*, La Baconnière, 1964.

Judith Robinson, *L'Analyse de l'esprit dans les Cahiers de Paul Valéry*, Corti, 1963.

Pierre Roulin, *Paul Valéry témoin et juge du monde moderne*, La Baconnière, 1964.

Francis Scarfe, *The Art of Paul Valéry*, Heinemann, 1954.

Jürgen Schmidt-Radefeldt, *Paul Valéry linguiste dans les Cahiers*, Klincksieck 1970.

Lisa Schroeder, *Valéry, La Jeune Parque, Versuch einer Interpretation*, Hamburg Kommissionverlag: Cram, de Gruyter, 1955.

Hans Sorensen, *La Poésie de Paul Valéry; Etude Stylistique sur La Jeune Parque*, Aarhus, 1944.

Norman Suckling, *Paul Valéry and the civilized mind*, Oxford, 1954.

F. Sutcliffe, *La Pensée de Paul Valéry*, Nizet, 1955.

Pierre-Olivier Walzer, *La Poésie de Valéry*, P. Cailler, 1953.

Charles G. Whiting, *Valéry jeune poète*, PUF, 1960.

INDEX